Voting Behaviour

Critical Political Studies
Edited by Jules Townshend

———

This series from Leicester University Press
offers lively and accessible critiques of orthodoxies,
old and new, within the discipline of politics.

Forthcoming titles in the series

Capitalism and Democracy in the Third World:
The Doctrine for Political Development
PAUL CAMMACK

Liberal Philosophy: A Critique of Key Concepts
MAUREEN RAMSAY

Analysing Public Policy
PETER JOHN

For more information on this series, or to submit a book proposal,
please contact the series editor:

Jules Townshend
Manchester Metropolitan University
Department of Social Science
Chatham/Undercroft Building
Cavendish Street
Manchester M15 6BR

Voting Behaviour
A Radical Critique

Helena Catt

Leicester University Press
London and New York

LEICESTER UNIVERSITY PRESS
A Cassell imprint
Wellington House, 125 Strand, London WC2R 0BB
127 West 24th Street, New York, NY 10011
First published in Great Britain 1996

British Library Cataloguing-in-Publication Data
A catalogue record for this book is available from The British Library.

Library of Congress Cataloging-in-Publication Data
Catt, Helena.
    Voting Behaviour : a radical critique / Helena Catt.
    p.   cm. – (Critical political studies)
    Includes bibliographical references and index.
    ISBN 0–7185–1473–4 (hardback). – ISBN 0–7185–2232–X (pbk.)
    1. Voting – Great Britain.   2. Elections – Great Britain.
    I. Title.   II. Series
    JN961.C37 1996
    324.941 – dc20   96–32411
                                                                              CIP

                ISBN 0–7185–1473–4 (hardback)
                      0–7185–2232–X (paperback)

Typeset by Chapter One (London)
Printed and bound in Great Britain by Redwood Books,
Trowbridge, Wiltshire

Contents

Acknowledgements

Most of the ideas in this book first saw the light of day in my doctoral thesis on tactical voting. Not only did my supervisor, Patrick Dunleavy, refrain from dismissing these early signs of dissent from the orthodoxy, he actively nourished them. For that early support and his continued encouragement, I am eternally grateful. My parents deserve a big thank you for the vital support, both financial and emotional, which they provided during my student years. My family also bears a wider responsibility for their early training in the desirability of questioning everything, especially orthodoxies, which has played a large part in my academic work. The series editor, Jules Townshend, and the people at Leicester University Press deserve thanks for providing an opportunity to write in a critical fashion. Their comments on the manuscript were of great help, as were those of other friends and colleagues who have been badgered into reading various versions. Although the part played by all of these people was important, as always I take sole responsibility for the ideas and words contained in these pages.

Helena Catt
Auckland, November 1995

1

Is There a Voting Behaviour Orthodoxy?

Voting is integral to liberal democratic government, so the question of why people vote as they do poses a fundamental puzzle for political scientists. Many different answers have been suggested, but there is little consensus on a solution. The fact that academics do not agree about how to explain the central question of voting behaviour does not mean that there is no voting behaviour orthodoxy. This chapter will follow three steps on the path to identifying the components that make up a voting behaviour orthodoxy in Britain. First, the evolution of the study of voting behaviour is outlined, paying attention to the various approaches that are used and the range of explanations that have been considered. In the second section the idea that there is 'fierce debate within tight confines' is outlined by looking at similarities between the different voting behaviour models. Common elements in both the way in which the problem is perceived and the methods used to answer it are covered. The final section elaborates the contention that these similarities can be called an orthodoxy. The following three chapters look at details of the orthodox position, and the concluding chapter outlines some alternative approaches.

The actual texts published in Britain are used to examine the general approach to voting behaviour. While Britain provides the focus for this book, much that is said about the orthodoxy is applicable to other countries. Similar models are applied to election data in a variety of countries, but publications usually relate to just one country. Academics borrow ideas across national frontiers, and interest in understanding voting behaviour is global, but analysis is country-specific. As studies of voting behaviour generally concentrate on one election, which they seek to explain, publications deal with the particular set of parties, policy platforms, leaders and political history in that country. So the same models and ideas are adapted by academics in different countries studying their own unique situation. There is a growing amount of cross-national work, but it tends to concentrate on one specific aspect of voting behaviour, such as the set of attitudes known as post-materialism or looking for differences between the attitudes of men and women – the gender gap. These studies take one group of voters or variables and compare them across the different political systems to look for patterns of similarity and difference. Elections are studied country by country, while particular aspects are compared across a range of countries.

How the Study of British Voting Behaviour Evolved

Around the world and across time, the right to vote has been fought for by groups who were excluded from the system, because enfranchisement is seen as a sign of acceptance and citizenship. Elections, where the people are periodically asked to choose the political decision-makers who will rule for a succeeding period, are at the centre of modern ideas of democratic control. Casting a vote is the main way in which people participate in the democratic process. An election is therefore a notable point in the political life of any democracy and the focus of much attention. Through the aggregation of many individual votes, the policy direction is set and the personalities who will rule are determined. It is hardly surprising that questions about how people vote and why they make the decisions they do when faced with a ballot paper have long intrigued those who follow politics. Examples of early approaches come from academics (see Baxter, 1866; Martin, 1874; Newmarch, 1857) and the media: *The Economist* magazine has included commentary on all elections in Britain (general and by-elections) this century.

Detailed study of the reasons for individual voting decisions, however, is relatively recent. Between the introduction of secret voting in 1872 and the development of opinion surveys and computers in the 1950s, obtaining information on individual voting decisions (let alone attitudes) was almost impossible. When voting was open, the detail of each person's vote was recorded along with facts about his social and economic position. With the introduction of secret voting this source of information was lost and no new source appeared until the introduction of opinion polls after the Second World War. The availability of computers that could deal with information about large numbers of people, and calculate statistics much faster than humans, meant that opinion poll information could be used to study the views of voters. So in recent decades, with the help of new technology, voting behaviour has become a popular area of political study among academics and lay people alike. Indeed, 'electoral politics is the forum of social research that is at the same time most interesting to and best understood by those who are not social scientists' (Franklin, 1985, p.2). The continued interest in, and topicality of, studies of voting behaviour is aided by the predictable frequency of elections. After each new election there are fresh data to analyse, and new ideas or explanations for the behaviour of the voters may be needed. The study of elections is never short of new examples.

Early work on voting behaviour in Britain concentrated on voters in individual constituencies. Benney and colleagues (1956) conducted panel surveys in the constituency of Greenwich, and Milne and MacKenzie (1958) did the same in Bristol North East. They were following a research design that was being used by researchers at the University of Columbia in New York. As expounded in *The People's Choice* (Lazarsfeld *et al.*, 1948) and later in *Voting* (Berelson *et al.*, 1954), the 'social determinism' approach or 'Columbia' agenda started with a desire to explain how individual voters make up their minds. These researchers pioneered the technique of asking a series of people in one district the same questions over a number of weeks (local panel surveys). By asking one person for his or her view on the same issue on three separate days, the analysts were able to look at the way each person behaves over time. This approach differs from a comparison of successive surveys, where different people are asked each time, because in the latter case we know how the overall views of each sample differ but not whether individuals have changed their opinions. The data that the Columbia researchers collected from the panel surveys were used to examine the influence on the voting decision of different 'actors', such as newspapers, family, workmates, the local campaign and local political leaders, over the course of the campaign. The research teams wanted to know if the people were interested in politics, and if they based their voting decisions on knowledge about the candidates and salient issues. They were particularly interested in influences on those people who changed their vote at successive elections, often called floating voters.

In both Britain and the United States floating voters were found to be uninterested in politics, the least informed and lacking strong views on important election issues. Both of the British survey teams discovered, as had the Americans, that only about a quarter of the people in the studies changed their voting intention during the campaign. Indeed, so many of those surveyed claimed that they had decided how to vote well before the campaign had begun, that the researchers concluded that voting is based on stable predispositions that are formed as a consequence of social location: 'People who work or live or play together are likely to vote for the same candidates' (Lazarsfeld et al., 1948, p.137). In Britain, class was seen as the most important type of social location, so that 'political allegiances are in fact formed along class lines' (Benney et al., 1956, p.120). The social group you belong to, be it defined by class, religion, race or whatever, determines whom you vote for, because 'during the campaign social groups imbue their individual members with the accepted political ideology of the group' (Lazarsfeld et al., 1948, p.147). Instead of finding politically interested citizens who weighed the merits of the parties and candidates at each election, the researchers found people who thought little about the specifics of the contest.

Throughout these studies, the emphasis was on looking at details of an individual decision in a specific local contest at that particular election. The surveys were carried out in one area so that locality-specific details of the campaign could also be gathered. The researchers were interested in looking at the effects of local newspapers, neighbourhood meetings and other local aspects of the campaign and electoral contest. But the findings suggested a lack of election-specific influences and instead more stable attachments to parties: 'the subjects in our study tended to vote as they always had, in fact as their families always had' (Lazarsfeld et al., 1948, p.xx). From these results it emerged that what was needed to understand voting in Britain (and the USA) was a nationwide survey not tied to a specific election campaign that would examine the stabilizing, long-term trends in partisanship. Stable tendencies rather than campaign choices were seen as important.

David Butler and Donald Stokes conducted the first set of British surveys in 1963, 1964, 1966, 1969 and 1970. They also used a panel element to study how individuals behaved over time, but the big change from previous studies was that they covered the whole country. Rather than concentrating on the specifics of one area, Butler and Stokes were interested in looking at nationwide patterns. They followed the research design that had been pioneered at the

University of Michigan, in response to the findings of the earlier research conducted in specific constituencies. The Michigan model, first outlined in *The American Voter* (Campbell *et al.*, 1960), focused on the stable, long-term patterns of partisanship, using nationwide sample surveys. The emphasis was no longer on the specific, but instead on general trends that prevailed across time and place. Stabilizing factors rather than agents of change were being investigated.

Social location, particularly class in Britain, was still a crucial factor in explaining voting behaviour, but suggestions about the way in which the two were linked formed an important new step. In the Michigan model social location is seen as determining who voters interact with, which will in turn influence their attachment to a political party. In other words, the class (or race or religion) you belong to will affect who you see and talk to about politics, which in turn helps to create a party attachment or partisan self-image. This attachment, now commonly known as party identification, is strong and long term. Party identification, once it has been acquired, acts as a filter on other information and ideas and determines how voters evaluate issues or politicians: 'The strength of relationship between party identification and the dimensions of partisan attitude suggests that responses to each element of national politics are deeply affected by the individual's enduring party attachment' (Campbell *et al.*, 1960, p.128). People may not always vote for the party they identify with, but they will have a long-term commitment to that party, which acts as a stabilizing force on patterns of voting over time. In Britain, class was clearly the main factor in a model of voting behaviour based on social location. With the Conservative and Labour parties winning the vast majority of votes and the dominance of the middle-class/working-class divide, the party identification model that linked class to party was intuitively appealing.

The series of nationwide surveys conducted by Butler and Stokes became the authoritative dataset, and *Political Change in Britain* (Butler and Stokes, 1969; 2nd edn, 1974) became the definitive text on British voting behaviour. 'By the early 1970s, therefore, the "two-class, two-party" model formed the textbook orthodoxy about British voters and elections' (Crewe and Norris, 1992, p.16). Although the creation of party identification was only part of *Political Change in Britain*, it was the section that attracted most attention because it contained more new ideas and a great deal of detail. Contrary to the early studies, little was said about short-term fluctuations as they were seen as minor, short-lived and making little difference to individuals' views or to the election result. The big puzzle with this new model was cross-class voting. The anomalies of working-class Conservatives or middle-class Labour voters were usually explained as being due to other social location effects such as religion, being in a rural community or having recently moved class (see Nordlinger, 1967; McKenzie and Silver, 1968). Social location and who people talk to were still central to explanations of cross-class voting; it was just that a group other than class provided the important political connection.

It was political events that shook the dominant position of the Michigan model in Britain. The growing level of votes cast for the Nationalist parties in Scotland and Wales, and for the Liberals across the country, in the 1970s, particularly in the 1974 elections, dented the two-party dominance that was central to the classic party identification model in Britain. Increased volatility also weakened the stability arguments. When people behave differently at successive elections, for example, voting Labour, then SNP, then Liberal, it is called volatility, because voters are volatile rather than predictable. If people change their vote, then explanations of stable attachments are no longer able to explain the result. The previously strong, long-term ties between voter and party appeared to be weakening, and this was termed class dealignment. As partisan ties weakened, short-term factors seemed to become more important in shaping voting behaviour. Reactions to the economic situation drew a great deal of attention from politicians, commentators and academics. This focus led to a new interest in 'issue voting' and 'pocketbook voting'. Analysis based on ideas of rational choice emerged, but no single model took over as the dominant explanation for the perceived deficiencies of the Michigan model. Instead, a number of different approaches were tried, most of which still included some aspect of social location effects.

In the 1970s, Bo Sarlvik and Ivor Crewe took over the British Election Survey (BES) series from Butler and Stokes. In *Decade of Dealignment* (Sarlvik and Crewe, 1983) they examined the impact of class on voters, plus an array of attitudes towards the issues, parties and leaders. They concluded that, 'the electorate became more ready to sway in response to short-term factors, especially the issues that were the cause of immediate concern' (p.337). In considering the attitudes of voters to various issues, researchers were drawing upon ideas from the rational choice model. Rather than concentrating on group membership, the rational choice model sees voters as individuals who make a decision on whether to vote and which party to vote for after careful assessment of the issues. First, voters determine their own views on the issues they see as most important, then how well these views match the positions of the parties and finally they evaluate how well each policy stance will be carried through. Sarlvik and Crewe included all three aspects of this rational choice model by asking each respondent how relevant the issue was to them personally (saliency), which party they preferred on that issue and how competent they thought each party was.

Hilde Himmelweit and colleagues in *How Voters Decide* (Himmelweit *et al.*, 1985) also concentrated on aspects of issue-based voting. Their initial study used data from a panel survey of boys who were tracked and periodically interviewed as they became adults. Although this study was not initiated with voting behaviour in mind, it did contain questions on how the boys/men felt about various political issues. The model that these researchers developed using the panel data on the boys was then tested using the BES datasets for 1970 to 1983. Taking classic rational choice ideas, the team developed a 'consumer' model of voting, where voters choose the party whose total package of offerings most attracts them, regardless of their assumed chance of success. It is the party as an amalgam of policies and people rather than any one policy that is critical. So voter perception of each party's stance is important, as is each voter's assessment of the relative importance of different issues.

At the same time, and outside of the BES series, others had been developing different lines of argument aimed at explaining the perceived dealignment between class and vote. Some, most notably Richard Rose and Ian McAllister (1986), considered refinements to the class structure to create core classes that still strongly predicted the votes of the two major parties. Rather than accept the idea that there had been a fundamental change in behaviour, they sought to refine the measurements that were used. They argued that class was still important, but it should not be defined on narrow occupation lines, as Butler and Stokes had done. In an attempt to define a new meaningful class structure they looked at other socio-economic aspects, such as type of housing tenure, education level, trade union membership and car ownership. Instead of seeing partisanship as something that is acquired then carried for life, they talked of a 'lifetime of learning' with people's views being influenced by their own changing circumstances and the shifts in the political arena as new parties and issues come and go.

The new model proposed by Patrick Dunleavy and Christopher Husbands (1985) also included ideas based on social determinants rather than attitudes as the main influence on voting. In redefining class they concentrated on the public–private division in production and consumption sectors. They argued that the type of education, housing, transport and health care a person consumes will affect their views on the role of government. Likewise, people working for private companies will have a different set of interests and views from those working for the state. Dunleavy and Husbands still saw the vote decision as a product of social location, but with a different map, adding consideration of the effects of political competition between parties and the way in which the situation is presented to voters. In particular, they stressed the role of the media in disseminating and explaining political information.

Taking a different approach and using census rather than survey data, Ron Johnston and colleagues, in *A Nation Dividing?* (Johnston *et al.*, 1988), investigated the geographical pattern of voting. They related differences in voting patterns between constituencies to other spatial patterns, such as class, functional regions, unemployment, council tenancy, agriculture and having parents from the New Commonwealth. For instance, they looked at the percentage of Conservative voters in each constituency and related it to the percentage of people who were managers or university graduates. They looked at both constituency-specific influences and regional cleavages or patterns. William Miller (1977) had also done work of this nature in correlating census data and voting data for constituency units from 1918 to 1974, and considering such variables as class, region, religion and patterns of candidature. In these studies, variables measuring social location are still seen as important, but these researchers employ different methods of analysis by looking at the relationship between variables at the level of the constituency rather than the individual voter.

In the 1980s, Anthony Heath, Roger Jowell and John Curtice took over the BES, with a resultant shift in emphasis. Rather than posit a new model, they sought to bring together the two previous models derived from this series of data (party identification and issue voting). They suggested in *How Britain Votes* (Heath *et al.*, 1985) that a three-party, five-class framework was appropriate (p.20). Using data from the full sweep of surveys in the series, Heath and his team rebutted the suggestion that dealignment had replaced long-term stability. Instead they argued that there had just been blips in what was otherwise a trendless fluctuation. These blips were due to changes in the party system caused by actions of the political élite, such as the creation of the SDP, rather than to changes within the electorate (p.35). In a later book, *Understanding Political Change* (1991), the same team used the election surveys from 1964 to 1987 to continue their examination of long-term trends. They concluded that '... while the social psychology of the voter may not have changed much, the social and political conditions under which the parties competed for votes in the 1980s have certainly been rather different from those of the 1960s' (Heath *et al.*, 1991, p.200).

In the late 1980s, William Miller, with a team of academics, returned to some of the interests of the Columbia model and conducted detailed studies of the campaign period. Data for *How Voters Change* (Miller *et al.*, 1990) were collected by re-interviewing people up to five times, including twice during the 1987 election campaign. The authors were then able to chart changes in the perceptions and views of individuals over time and so show the extent of individual volatility. By using these data on day by day replies from voters on their views, and details of television coverage, the team was '... able to distinguish between coincidence and causation' (Miller *et al.*, 1990, p.vii). They studied the interplay of partisan views, attitudes, political perceptions and the political context to ascertain the different roles of long- and short-term influences on an individual's voting decision.

The new approaches that aimed to address the problems of the Michigan model tapped a variety of sources, in terms of ideas and data. Some, such as Sarlvik and Crewe or Himmelweit, adopted rational choice ideas based on perceptions of 'economic man'. Others veered back to the beginning of the cycle to resume the Columbia interest in looking at short-term, localized effects or to concentrate on locational position in relation to group interest. Meanwhile Heath and colleagues argued that continuity was still dominant. After the turbulent years of the 1970s and early 1980s 'the emphasis is once more on the remarkable continuity of party systems and the unchanging psychology of the voter' (Crewe and Norris, 1992, p.19). What all of these works have in common is their starting point. They all seek to explain why dealignment occurred and why old patterns of stability have weakened.

The works mentioned in this brief overview of the evolution of the study of voting behaviour in Britain do not comprise an exhaustive list. However, they serve to outline the basic strands of inquiry. The key texts from which extensive examples will be taken are: *Political Change in Britain* (Butler and Stokes, 1974); *Decade of Dealignment* (Sarlvik and Crewe, 1983); *How Voters Decide* (Himmelweit *et al.*, 1985); *Voters Begin to Choose* (Rose and McAllister, 1986); *British Democracy at the Crossroads* (Dunleavy and Husbands, 1985); *How Britain Votes* (Heath *et al.*, 1985); and *Understanding Political Change* (Heath *et al.*, 1991). Other important works in key areas will be mentioned as specific aspects of the different models are explored later in the book.

Ideas about voting behaviour have changed markedly over the last several decades. Twenty years ago most of those studying voting behaviour would have agreed on the centrality of party identification. Now, a meeting of all the academics who study voting behaviour in Britain would result in major arguments over which model is best and what variables are most important. The strong influence from the USA is evident in the three main sets of ideas that have been influential in the changing study of voting behaviour. The Columbia research agenda studied the short-term influences on voters, but instead found strong group influences. The Michigan model stressed group membership and emphasized the stabilizing role of party identification. The third set of ideas is looser, but shares the common desire to explain why fewer voters follow stable voting patterns than had previously been the case. Rational choice ideas based on voting due to views on key issues have played an important part in this latest research agenda.

Paralleling the change in explanations for the voting decision have been differences in the statistical methods used. In the main texts, along with the common techniques of cross-tabulation tables and multiple regression, a vast range of procedures can be found, including: the 'Index of Determination' (Rose and McAllister, 1986, p.38); the 'index of dissimilarity' (Heath *et al.*, 1985, p.108); 'Mostellerised' flow of the vote matrixes (Johnston *et al.*, 1988, p.116); log-linear analysis (Dunleavy and Husbands, 1985, p.134; Heath *et al.*, 1991, p.67); and Multiple Scalogram Analysis (Himmelweit *et al.*, 1985, p.36). It is no wonder that Denver (1989, pp.6–21) starts his introduction to voting behaviour with an outline of basic statistical techniques.

The most appropriate technique to use is the source of much argument between research teams. Some writers use an alternative technique to challenge an idea in a rival's study: 'a discriminate analysis using the same data set has falsified that claim' (Johnston et al., 1988, p.59). Others recognize that using different techniques on the same data will alter the findings: 'There are a number of methodological reasons which could account for the differences between our results and Franklin's' (Heath et al., 1991, p.43), or 'given our stricter definition of class, it is not surprising that our detailed figures ... are rather different from the ones quoted by Butler and Kavanagh' (Heath et al., 1985, p.45). Statistical methods have become part of the central argument about how best to explain voting behaviour.

To match the range of techniques used, a variety of datasets has also been employed. While many texts use the central bank of British Election Surveys (Butler and Stokes, 1974; Sarlvik and Crewe, 1983; Rose and McAllister, 1986; Heath et al., 1985, 1991), this is by no means the only source of data. Some works are based on custom-built surveys (Dunleavy and Husbands, 1985; Miller et al., 1991) or use data from surveys conducted for other purposes, such as media opinion polls (Rose and McAllister, 1986), different academic programmes (Himmelweit et al., 1985) or regular census exercises (Johnston et al., 1988). Techniques for collecting information on voters also cover the range from postal surveys, through telephone polls, to face-to-face interviews, with a common panel element built into many of them.

While voting behaviour texts now display great variety there is still general agreement about the importance of *Political Change in Britain* by Butler and Stokes (1969, 1974). Not only does their book pre-date most other major works on British voting (although as has been noted above it is not the first) and draw on the first in the series of nationwide election studies, but it also sets out the basis for later debate. One of the key textbooks on British politics explains that 'in-depth analysis of the British electorate has a very short history. The first nationwide study of the British electorate, *Political Change in Britain*, was published less than three decades ago and most current work addresses themes raised in that volume' (Dunleavy et al., 1990, p.339). In later works there is a clear feeling that they all make connections back to this seminal work and must all be influenced by it. It is widely recognized that, 'once a theory or model gains influence it does more than offer an explanation for the observations made. It indicates to future researchers what is figure and what is ground, i.e. what needs explanation and what might be taken for granted or ignored' (Himmelweit *et al.*, 1985, p.5). In most subsequent works on voting behaviour the earlier orthodoxy was used as a starting point. For instance Sarlvik and Crewe said that, '*Political Change in Britain* laid a foundation for research on voting and public opinion of such originality and comprehensiveness that almost every path that we have followed in our research has taken their book as a starting point' (1983, p.x). Later works either continue the arguments used by Butler and Stokes, seek to explain why party identification is weakening or refute the dominance of stable partisanship in the first place. So, although *Political Change in Britain* is no longer the unchallenged model for explaining voting in Britain, it is still very influential.

During the 1960s and early 1970s the orthodox position followed the party identification model put forward by Butler and Stokes. By the late 1970s there was some talk that this 'old orthodoxy' had been replaced with a new one that centred around ideas of issue voting. More recent works have either tried to tie the two models together or sought other explanations. From a situation of having an orthodox line following the Michigan model there are now numerous accepted positions. Indeed, there now seem to be many orthodoxies existing at the same time. Within one book, a whole variety of orthodoxies may be mentioned. The following quotes all come from *Understanding Political Change* (Heath *et al.*, 1991): 'The orthodoxy established by Butler and Stokes in the 1960s… '(p. 62); 'dissent from the new orthodoxy [class secularization]…' (p.63); 'the orthodox interpretations of the relationship between Labour and the working class' (p.103). In recent years there has been some heated debate about the existence of a voting behaviour orthodoxy (for example, Dunleavy, 1990; Crewe and Norris, 1992). Now the more prevalent view, the orthodoxy if you like, is that there is not an orthodox view on voting behaviour in Britain. Crewe and Norris argue that, 'a wide range of work flourished in the 1980s, diverse in method and substance, shaped not by a rigid orthodoxy but by a broad research agenda' (1992, p.20).

Fierce Debate within Tight Confines

At first glance the whole area of voting behaviour seems to be enjoying energetic debate. However, scratch the surface and the impression of wide variety and disagreement fades. There is much debate and controversy, but it is contained within a framework of accepted working practices. The rules of the game are recognized and adhered to by the competing research teams. These hidden but acknowledged boundaries to the debate cover both the central question to be answered and the way to do so: concept and method. Throughout the range of competing works certain aspects of voting behaviour are scrutinized, but other areas are ignored or confined to occasional footnotes. A strong agreement on what is interesting and which questions need to be answered seems to exist. There is a shared conception of what the study of voting behaviour should look at. There are also certain interpretational assumptions that are followed rather than questioned. This continuity of working assumptions holds even for authors who are highly critical of the findings or methods of previous works. Much is made of the range of new models and inventive approaches but, when you look for them, the similarities between the different models and the continuity of approach are as striking as the differences. The rest of this section will concentrate on outlining common strands or themes and accepted working practices.

One important assumption that is uniformly accepted is the central question that is to be addressed in studies of voting behaviour. Behind the classic work of the Michigan model was the basic idea that the phenomenon to be explained was the level of vote received by each party at a given election. This remains the basic question that is addressed (for example, Sarlvik and Crewe, 1983, p.x; Johnston *et al.*, 1988, p.1; Heath *et al.*, 1991, p.1). Hence studies often focus on a specific election rather than considering groups of voters. Early studies examined the people who voted for each party to find common social features or attitudes that could then be used to predict the size of the future vote for the party. Or from the other direction, an individual's vote for a particular party was explained by the person's attitudes or background characteristics. In many ways the dealignment agenda became necessary because previous models were no longer satisfactorily answering this question. Later works questioned the issue-based model, but they still sought to answer the original question posed by Butler and Stokes: why do political parties receive varying numbers of votes at successive elections? Some may complain that this is the obvious question to answer when studying voting behaviour, but there are other questions that could equally be addressed in a study of voting, as will be outlined in chapters 2 and 5.

While using different models to try to answer this central question, two dominant interpretations of the act of voting are maintained. Implicit in the usual approach is the idea that a vote for a party is a sign of general support for all, or most of, what that party stands for and would do in government. So it is assumed that all voters for one party agree with the party, and each other, about central aspects of politics. Not only are voters assumed to base their decisions on positive feelings towards the party they vote for, but there is the added idea that a vote indicates the voter's endorsement of what the party stands for. This accepted interpretation of the meaning of a vote has important consequences for what is studied and what is ignored within the study of voting behaviour (Catt, 1990). Allied to the assumption that a vote is a sign of support is the idea that voters behave in a rational way when choosing the best party. Notions of economic gain, group promotion and utility maximization are used to explain why a group of voters backs one party rather than another. Writers argue about the form such a rational decision takes, but all assume voters are choosing the option they think will be best for themselves.

A third set of assumptions concerns the aspects of voting behaviour that should be carefully studied. Later works follow the parameters that were drawn by Butler and Stokes. For example:

...because in the early studies those not identified with any party were found to be badly informed, little involved in politics and disinterested in the outcomes of elections, for many years political scientists devoted hardly any attention to them. Instead research concentrated on those who identified with the major parties, thereby exaggerating the degree of polarisation of attitudes among the electorate. (Himmelweit *et al.*, 1985, p.192)

On the other side of the coin, certain areas are accepted as ignorable: '...Liberals could have little influence on overall patterns of voting; hence, a case could be made for setting them aside. The pioneering Butler and Stokes (1969) study of British voting often did just that' (Rose and McAllister, 1986, p.36). Concentration on major party voters or party identifiers and those who have an interest in politics is widespread among studies of voting behaviour.

Assumptions about the relevance of the election context have also continued. The most notable example is the lack of comment about the effect of the first-past-the-post electoral system on election results and party fortunes. Voters are reacting to the set of choices that are presented at an election rather than to questions about their ideal political future. But studies of voting behaviour take the ways in which the system frames electoral choices as a given and therefore not in need of comment. In a similar way, Dunleavy and Husbands decry the tendency started by Butler and Stokes, and continued by other political scientists, of separating psephology (the study of voting) from a study of the political dynamics and context (1985, p.xviii). The Michigan concentration on general trends that were not dependent on time or place has also persisted. Many of the works cover a number of elections and seek trends across them rather than election-specific aspects. Again this desire for general trends rather than specific details works to hide system effects. A fourth common theme, then, is to study elections as isolated events with little reference to other aspects of the political world that affect voters.

So far the common aspects have related to the way in which the study of voting behaviour is perceived, but there are also similarities in the methods used to conduct the analysis. Again Butler and Stokes set the British agenda, although they were following the methods used by the Michigan team. Nationwide surveys conducted just after an election are the normal source of data used in the study of voting behaviour. Respondents are randomly chosen to provide geographic spread so that patterns that apply to the whole country can be discerned. The resulting dataset contains information on the views, beliefs and socio-economic background of well over a thousand voters. The nature of these data also leads to the routine use of techniques that give information about large groups (aggregate data). The ever-increasing availability of powerful computers enables statistical techniques to be used that can utilize such vast amounts of data. Such data and techniques aid the discovery of widespread trends rather than the study of small groups. The basic common assumption about which method to use in explaining voting behaviour is that aggregate data from large nationwide surveys are needed.

A second methodological assumption that almost reaches a reified status is the need for continuity over time in the questions that people are asked in a survey. Academics in one team will replicate questions used by earlier researchers to provide them with a basis for comparison. Within the mainstream voting studies community (and indeed other survey-based fields) there is a perceived imperative in keeping the same questions and using the same basis of categorization. In part, this practice is reinforced by the terms of the main funding body for BES, who require panel surveys and the precise replication of question wording in successive surveys (Crewe and Norris, 1992, p.6). The stress on continuity again reinforces the impact of Butler and Stokes, as they wrote many of the questions that are now slavishly copied.

Having gathered the data, there are more assumptions about the way in which they should be analysed. Because of the centrality of the question of why each party gains a certain level of the vote, analysts concentrated on discovering which variables relate to the party voted for. Vote is the variable to be explained, in statistical terms it is called the dependent variable. A great deal has been done, and some very potent statistical techniques used, to determine which variables, be they related to social location or attitudes, best correlate with voting for each party. But the same energy and method have not been consistently employed in explaining why these variables affect the vote. As Miller points out:

social groups have been very relevant to partisan choices but the extent of that relevance has been determined by party appeals to the electorate. It has not been automatic. For most voters in mainland Britain social divisions have not been so deep that there were any prescribed or proscribed choices among the three major parties. (1977, p.xii)

While some explanations are offered for the discovered correlation, little detailed work is done trying to prove the reasons for the connection between class (or attitude or economic situation, etc.) and the vote cast. Similarly, little has been said, since the works on cross-party voting (mentioned above), about those who do not fit the general patterns. As Scarbrough argues:

it has to be the work of the next generation of electoral studies to move the focus from description to explanation, from good record keeping to a secure grasp of the motive forces underlying partisan decisions. Elections are too important to the direction of political life for election surveys to rest on mapping the contours of social life and the vicissitudes of political opinion. (1987, pp.242–3)

The working practice of describing the common attributes of voters for each (major) party has played a central role in the evolution of the study of voting behaviour in Britain.

At every step in the study of voting behaviour in Britain there are common assumptions across the competing teams of researchers. The central question that needs to be answered and the way to go about that quest, both in terms of approach and methods, are shared among writers in the field. Ideas about what aspects and variables are to be included and what can safely be ignored are very similar across the central texts. In methodological terms data are collected and analysed in the same way. While the details within the models differ, so that the explanatory powers of different variables are stressed, all of the writers are staying within a restricted framework. The fierce debate among those who study voting behaviour takes place within the tight confines laid down in *Political Change in Britain* (Butler and Stokes, 1969).

The Voting Behaviour Orthodoxy?

As has been shown, there are many different ideas about how voting behaviour in Britain can be explained, but the studies share certain key assumptions. The primary question, then, is whether or not the similarities are sufficient to justify the description of a voting behaviour orthodoxy. An orthodoxy is the received or established doctrines or opinions:

Orthodox ...

1. Holding right or correct opinions, i.e. such as are currently accepted as correct, or are in accordance with some recognised standard ...

2. Of opinions or doctrines: Right, correct, true, in accordance with what is accepted or authoritatively established as the true view or right practice; ... orig[in] in theological and ecclesiastical doctrine ...

3. In accordance with what is regarded as proper or 'correct'; conventional; approved.

(*Oxford English Dictionary*, 1993, p. 951)

The term is often associated with Church groups such as Orthodox Jews or the Russian Orthodox Church. In a theological context orthodox people are those who are more traditional or hardline in belief and practice. Often it is the way in which things are done as well as what is believed that constitutes an orthodox position. Loosely, the orthodox way is the traditional, accepted way of thinking and behaving. The inclusion of method as well as ideas is important in establishing a voting behaviour orthodoxy, as much of what ties the models together relates to the way in which the studies are undertaken.

Political Change in Britain (Butler and Stokes, 1969) used to be considered the orthodox work because of the widespread accept-ance that its model of voting behaviour (party identification) explained why people vote as they do. In the academic world an orthodoxy is frequently centred around the work of one person or the ideas contained in one book. When the consensus about the accuracy of the party identification model broke down, largely due to an increase in the number of voters who changed how they voted from one election to the next (volatility), no single model took over as the definitive one. Instead there was a wide range of suggested explanations for the way people vote and particularly as to why stable partisanship was no longer the key. Thus the new accepted or orthodox position was that there was no orthodox view to explain the behaviour of British voters. Rather than a single model there was a field of competing ideas. So, suggesting that a British voting behaviour orthodoxy exists is, in some ways, challenging the exist-ing orthodox position.

Unusually, the voting behaviour orthodoxy described here does not consist of one model contained in one book. Rather it refers to a general approach, a way of proceeding, an outline of the questions that need to be asked and what can be ignored or taken for granted. As the previous section showed, there are a number of important strands that run through the major voting behaviour texts covering both the conceptual and the methodological sides of analysis. Taken together, these accepted norms are so pervasive that they constitute an orthodox approach. As it is the working assumptions that all who study voting behaviour automatically follow, rather than one model of voting, that constitute the orthodoxy, its effect is both stronger and more difficult to detect. The next three chapters will examine the different strands of the orthodoxy showing evidence of their existence and effect.

Norms relating to the way in which the central question within voting behaviour is perceived and understood form the basis of Chapter 2. The orthodox approach covers the aims of the study of voting behaviour; normal interpretations of key ideas; and what aspects should be studied. The main aim is to explain the level of vote received by each party and to discover general explanatory trends that apply across the country. The normal interpretation sees the voting decision as a rational choice of the best option and a vote as an indication of support for that party. In the course of study, certain groups, such as third parties or ill-informed voters, are sidelined and context effects connected to the two-party system and the first-past-the-post electoral system are ignored. This orthodox approach to the study of voting behaviour channels attention towards the common characteristics of those who habitually vote for the main parties.

Technical or methodological aspects are examined in Chapter 3, as the collection of data, as well as their use, is affected by the orthodoxy. Information on voters' attitudes and behaviour is collected using national surveys with an emphasis on continuity of questions. Therefore new topics and innovative forms of questioning respondents are not easily included. Analysis concentrates on aggregate data rather than voters as individuals, and statistical analysis tends to employ 'number crunching' techniques, which all adds to the tendency to look for general patterns of behaviour. Investigation treats the party that was voted for as the variable to be explained, rather than dividing voters into any other types of meaningful category. This methodology shapes the orthodoxy as much as the shared approach does. With a common pool of data and similar techniques, analysis is again confined within set parameters.

Chapter 4 examines three specialized areas within the study of voting behaviour in relation to the impact of the orthodoxy. Party identification and class voting are both central ideas, but both also arouse much heated debate. Authors argue about the interpretation, measurement and relevance of these concepts. However, these arguments, like the broader ones, are shaped and channelled by the orthodoxy. Another highly contentious theory is that of a neighbourhood or context effect on the voters. This notion is rarely mentioned in the texts that form the orthodoxy. Here, the impact of the orthodoxy is to sideline a potential explanatory model that does not fit within the norms of interpretation.

The study of voting behaviour has changed a great deal over the years with a succession of different models aimed at explaining the changing fortunes of political parties at the ballot box. However, across the competing models much has stayed the same, and this forms the orthodoxy. While arguing about which variables best explain voting behaviour, academics have maintained the working practices and parameters established by the Michigan model. There are common ideas about the central question, areas to study and methods of investigation. The rest of this book looks at various aspects of this orthodox position and seeks to show how the accepted procedures operate. Throughout, the links back to Butler and Stokes and the commonalities will be highlighted. Having established that each aspect of the orthodoxy exists, it is critically examined in light of its effect on the study of voting behaviour in Britain. The texts and examples used are specific to Britain, but much of the orthodox approach relates to other countries that have followed the Michigan model because of a shared ancestry of ideas. So the challenge to the orthodoxy is two-fold: to show that there is an orthodoxy and to suggest what is being missed because of this approach.

2

Aims, Interpretation and Parameters

Explaining the level of vote received by each party is the central aim of voting behaviour according to the orthodox approach. As outlined in Chapter 1, the orthodoxy covers not only the perceived aims of the study of voting behaviour, but also norms of interpretation of key ideas and what details should be studied. Here, four aspects of the orthodoxy are considered in more detail. The assumptions that a vote is a sign of support for that party, and that voters rationally choose the best option, were identified as part of the orthodoxy in Chapter 1. These norms of interpretation are among the most prevalent but hidden aspects of the orthodoxy and so will be considered in detail. Three specific parts of the normal interpretation are covered: choosing the best option; vote as a sign of support; and rational voters. Another crucial aspect of the orthodox approach is the agreement on what can be ignored when studying elections. One group of voters who are routinely neglected are those who are seen as ill-informed or irrational. So looking at ideas of rational voters covers both the orthodox interpretation and ideas on what to study. Another major area that is deemed outside the study of voting behaviour in the orthodoxy is the effect of the political system. The way in which system effects are neglected will be the fourth part of the orthodoxy to be considered in this chapter.

When looking in detail at these four aspects, two steps are taken. Establishing that there is a common approach forms the first part of the challenge to the orthodoxy. So, to illustrate the prevalence of each part of the orthodoxy, quotations from the central voting behaviour texts are cited. The effects of the orthodoxy are then discussed, in particular those aspects of voting behaviour which are missed because of the common working practices. This suggestion that the orthodoxy has undesirable effects forms the second part of the challenge. The final section of this chapter considers some examples of voting behaviour that do not fit within the orthodox approach. Looking at the ways in which negative, protest and tactical voting have been treated illustrates the combined effect of the orthodox aims, interpretation and parameters of study.

In Chapter 1 the orthodoxy was described as covering the perceived aims of the study of voting behaviour, normal interpretation and what should be studied, but in this chapter only aspects of interpretation and areas of coverage are examined. This emphasis on the normal interpretation is due primarily to its influence on the study of voting behaviour. Other aspects of the orthodoxy described in Chapter 1 are also less controversial. Agreement on the central aim of looking for general trends is widespread. The shift from the Columbia to the Michigan research agenda was characterized by a change towards finding general trends and concentrating on groups rather than individuals. The partisan research agenda was not the total break from the Michigan model that the Michigan model was from the Columbia model. The move to the Michigan agenda changed focus and methodology, while the move away from the Michigan agenda kept the nationwide focus and same basic methodology. The shift from the Columbia to the Michigan model was a switch in the focus and central question: from concentrating on local factors and the campaign, to looking for general trends not reliant upon election specifics. The progression from the Michigan model to the partisan dealignment agenda looked only for some different solutions to solve the problems found with the Michigan model. The first change said we need a totally new focus to deal with the findings of the previous model. The second said we need to do some remedial work and fill in some gaps now opening in the previous model. Although later works are not following the Michigan agenda, they take that model as a starting point and have been influenced by it.

What Do Voters Decide?

As Denver explains, we study elections to, among other things, '...discover how citizens make their voting decisions...' (1989, p.3), but he does not specify what decision is being made. Butler and Stokes (1974) recognize a variety of voting decisions, such as tactical voting (p.327) or fitting in with the social milieu or group (p.80). They suggest that at its basic level, '... the electorate attempts to use the ballot to achieve things it cares about' (p.28). However, much of the variety covered by Butler and Stokes has not been maintained in later works. A choice of 'the best party for them' is seen as the main decision facing voters. The unstated assumption is that voters are deciding which party they like best and that they then indicate the result of their decision by voting for that party. Nowhere is this explicitly spelt out but it is nevertheless the central assumption.

Early works did not necessarily see the vote as the result of a decision. There is some suggestion that in the party identification model '... it made little sense to think of the voter as "deciding" to vote for one party or another' (Denver, 1989, p.43), because 'party preference was a matter of heredity and habit, not decision-making' (Crewe and Norris, 1992, p.14). Nevertheless, voting, whether a decision or not, was an indication of preference. The issue-based models see the vote as a definite decision based on policy options. Again the decision is which party is best, and 'Voting masochists, out to select a party which would make matters worse, have no place in these [decision] models nor do voters who choose at random' (Himmelweit et al., 1985, p.114). Later works are scathing about the consumer model, saying it is wrong because it sees the vote as being based on a single conscious decision. These critics say that their analysis shows 'voting choices are not made on the basis of a conscious weighing in the balance of alternative policies', instead 'the fit between the general character of the party and the voter's own general ideology ... best accounts for electoral choice' (Heath et al., 1985, p.99). So the disagreement is about which factors are balanced in the decision. They are not disputing that each voter is deciding which party they 'like the best'.

Often, the suggestion of difference is in terms of how the decisions are reached rather than which decision is reached. For instance, Sarlvik and Crewe (1983) comment that they cannot expect their model to predict or explain all votes, because there are a vast array of reasons why voters make a particular decision, not all related to the issues used (p.268). Or Dunleavy and Husbands (1985), who make the fine distinction between decision and choice: 'However, as we set out to show in this volume, there is no simple sense in which voters decide. Citizens choose within options that are predefined for them by the process of party competition' (p.xviii). Nevertheless what is being chosen or decided is still unspecified. But for the models to make sense it must be that the voter is looking for the 'best' party.

The general practice of analysing all of those who vote for a party and determining what it is they have in common or what they like about the party, also assumes a vote for the 'best party' from all the voters. Looking at the group who voted for a given party as homogeneous in their election decision assumes that they all voted for the party they had decided was the best. Analysts assume that the members of the groups have a shared liking for their chosen party, and then try to determine what else the group members have in common that makes them feel that way.

Other types of decisions

While psephologists do mention other types of voting decisions, the concentration is clearly on which party is best. Arguments centre around the definition of 'best'. In its broadest sense, 'best' can mean 'least worst' and so covers negative voting, or it can mean 'fits my needs now' and so could cover a tactical vote. However, 'best' is usually taken in the narrower sense of 'most liked'. The old fruit-bowl analogy can be used to illustrate the range of motivations that can lie behind the choice of one particular option.

In the classic fruit-bowl situation, a person takes an apple from the extensive selection of fruit on offer and so is assumed to like apples best. However, my selection of an apple may be for a variety of other reasons. I may like grapes best, but there are none in the fruit-bowl: Scottish Nationalist voters in a constituency with no SNP candidate. I may like oranges best, but as those on offer have been sprayed with pesticides, I take my second best, apples, to uphold my personal pro-organic growing beliefs: pro-abortion Liberal-Democrats with an anti-abortion candidate they will not vote for. I may hate having to peel fruit and take an apple as it is the only one present that does not need peeling: voters who think a local connection is important, voting for the local dentist when all other candidates are carpet-baggers. I may like bananas best, but the one I had yesterday was rotten, so I take an apple: normal Conservative voters who switch to Plaid Cymru due to a recent disliked action by the Conservatives. I may usually eat cherries, but feel like a change today, and the apples look particularly shiny and crunchy, so I pick an apple: life-long Labour voters tired of the behaviour of the local candidate and impressed by the campaign of the Green Party, so they vote for the latter. The list could be continued, but these examples suffice to show that a wide variety of motivations can lie behind the picking of a particular option. Witnessing the choice is not enough to understand its true meaning.

For a single voting model to proceed, an assumption has to be made that all voters are doing the same thing, for only then can they be modelled. If voters are doing a variety of things, making different types of decisions, then a range of models are needed to cover the different decisions. There is a wide range of decisions that need to be considered. Rather than choosing the most-liked party, the vote could be a negative or protest or tactical vote. A voter may be interested in the choice of the best local candidate or the best party for government. A voter may want to stand up and be counted or desire to influence the result. Despite the wide range of ways in which voters may regard the election decision, the orthodoxy assumes that all are choosing the best option, and the other decision types are not taken seriously or integrated into the core voting behaviour models. As we cannot know that all (or even most) voters are choosing the best option, then a model of voting behaviour that only considers such a decision is bound to be incomplete.

Himmelweit's team asked in their title, 'How voters decide', but surely the more important and prior question is, 'What do voters decide?' If we understood why some voters choose their most-liked party and some are motivated by strong dislike or the desire to protest or to pick the best local candidate, then we would be better able to go on and determine how each vote is arrived at. Election studies generally try to explain why parties gain a different level of the vote at successive elections. More recently some have questioned the different level of vote won by a party for local, parliamentary and European elections. The orthodox approach is to look for changes in the way each party is perceived. Perhaps it would be useful to examine the type of decision that voters feel they are making at each election. Differing levels of vote for a party at different types of elections may be primarily due to the different ways in which voters approach the voting decision.

Is a Vote Always a Sign of Support?

As voters are assumed to see the voting decision as being a choice of the best option, then the vote, once cast, is taken as a sign of support for that party. This part of the orthodox interpretation of voting behaviour is equally subtle and pervasive. Whatever the voting decision, a vote is a mark of preference at a given time and place. But preference is often read as support, even though in dictionary terms the two are quite different. 'Preference' is 'the act of choosing, favouring or liking one above another', while 'support' is 'to uphold, to back-up, to supply with means of living' (Chambers, 1977).

Party identification, although not the only idea in the seminal work by Butler and Stokes, is the predominant idea to be used by other writers. Stated simply, '... most electors think of themselves as supporters of a given party in a lasting sense, developing what may be called a "partisan self-image"' (1974, p.39). Hidden within this description is the genesis of part of the orthodox interpretation: the use of the word 'support'. In this context, the word is employed in the usual sense of support meaning 'a strong commitment to'. This use of the idea of support is illustrated by Butler and Stokes when they suggest that:

As long-established actors on the political stage it is natural that the parties should have become objects of mass loyalty or identification. ... A prot-agonist in the political drama can evoke from the electoral audience a response at the polling station which has mainly to do with the values of having one's heroes prevail. ... We shall not probe very far into the realms of personality in this book, but we have no doubts that such factors supply part of the motives of electors who find intrinsic values in supporting a given party. (pp.36–7)

However, 'support' has also been used in a more general sense, by most psephologists, including Butler and Stokes themselves: 'Indeed, in the five intervals of change that we have examined in the 1960s, there were never as much as two-thirds of the public positively supporting the same party at two successive points of time' (1974, p.268). Here support means the giving of a vote, and has no implications of sustained interest as the earlier usage did. This mixing of a specific idea of support as a commitment and a more general use of support to mean a vote is one of the most important and subtle aspects of the orthodox approach.

Use of support to mean vote is widespread. A striking example can be found in *How Britain Votes*, where the data are claimed to show that 'support for the Conservative and Labour parties follows very similar lines to those of the class values', but the table is titled 'Class and Vote...' (Heath *et al.*, 1985, p.20). Clearly, support and vote are being used as synonyms. Both Dunleavy and Husbands

(1985, p.183) and Johnston's team (Johnston *et al.*, 1988, p.156) use the percentage of the vote for each party in each constituency, but then talk about levels of party support. Other examples abound, including most of the teams studied here (Heath *et al.*, 1991, p.173; Himmelweit *et al.*, 1985, p.41; Rose and McAllister, 1986, p.140; Sarlvik and Crewe, 1983, p.45). Rose and McAllister stretch the meaning of sustained support even further when they report that the '... parties could each claim the support of nearly half the electorate in the Gallup Poll' (1986, p.1). If support is equated with party identification, then it cannot be used as a synonym for voting, let alone the off-the-cuff response to an opinion poll.

Use of support as a more sustained idea is also to be found in the literature: 'In 1983 those socialized to support Labour were divided into two substantial groups, lifelong Labour voters and defectors from a Labour tradition' (Rose and McAllister, 1986, p.114). Although this use of support is less widespread than its use as a synonym for vote, it is found in other texts (for example Dunleavy and Husbands, 1985, p.98; Heath *et al.*, 1991, p.38; Johnston *et al.*, 1988, p.49). However, sometimes the word has to be qualified to show that real support, not just a vote, is meant. So we read about 'faithful supporters' (Himmelweit *et al.*, 1985, p.161); a 'hard core of supporters, with a firm sense of party allegiance' (Sarlvik and Crewe, 1983, p.334); and 'committed supporters' (Heath *et al.*, 1985, p.121). Some develop different terms instead, such as 'loyal voters' (Johnston *et al.*, 1988, pp.192–4), 'loyalists' (Heath *et al.*, 1985, p.110), 'identifiers' (Heath *et al.*, 1991, p.13) or 'committed partisans' (Rose and McAllister, 1986, p.150).

There are also examples of support being used both as a synonym for voting and to describe party adherence in the same paragraph:

but both parties also drew a substantial part of their **voting support** from among voters with a much weaker sense of attachment to the party for which they cast their votes and from the 'middle ground' of voters with more or less evenly balanced policy preferences. About one-tenth of the electorate is made up of voters who have no sense that they are **supporters of either of the parties**. [emphasis added] (Sarlvik and Crewe, 1983, p.306)

Confusion can arise when the authors do not specify which form of support is meant: 'Although the majority of floating major party voters liked the party they supported, their attitudes were less favourable than those of the consistent voters. ... In general, supporters of both parties were more favourable towards the Liberals than the opposition' (Himmelweit *et al.*, 1985, p.41). Does this refer to major party floaters liking the party they vote for or the party they identify with, and are the Liberals seen favourably by those who vote for the major parties or those who identify with the major parties? The meaning of the argument is quite different for the alternative interpretations of support.

There are signs that many of the authors covered here do regard a vote as primarily a sign of support, either because 'in most studies of electoral behaviour the fundamental assumption is usually made that people vote for the party they like best' (Heath *et al.*, 1991, p.52) or 'to the extent that a vote cast in an election means anything beyond an expression of trust in a party or an endorsement of a party's general aims . . . .' (Sarlvik and Crewe, 1983, p.202). However Sarlvik and Crewe (1983) also recognize that 'few voters actually cast a vote of deliberate support for the policies of their chosen party on all the issues' (p.202) and that 'an increasing portion of the voters cast their votes without any strong sense of allegiance to the party they choose to vote for in a particular election' (p.337).

So pervasive is the vote-as-support assumption underlying previous studies that it is rarely, if ever, made explicit. In setting out to explain why parties attract votes it is assumed that the voter supports that party. When support is frequently used as a synonym for a vote, then the connotations of 'support as sustaining' will be subconsciously applied to the vote. Therefore, the vote is increasingly decoded as a sign of commitment. Party identification theory did explicitly take a vote as a sign of commitment. However, subsequent rivals and critics tended to accept this assumption while attacking the rest of the model, and in later works the premise that a vote can be decoded as support is unstated. It is this basic assumption that vote equals support that causes the problems.

The effect of vote = support

When all votes are assumed to be given as a sign of support, other 'messages' or motivations are missed. The most obvious examples are a protest vote and a tactical vote. The former is meant to show disquiet with the party normally voted for, the latter aims to prevent the election of a disliked party. In neither case is the recipient of the vote receiving a sign of endorsement, just a preference given the present situation. Exactly what type of decision a voter makes at election time has already been discussed. Another aspect of deciphering voting decisions that is missed because of the vote as support assumption, is the relevance of negative feelings. While some writers, most noticeably Crewe, do incorporate ideas of negative partisanship into their work, this is usually combined with 'positive partisanship' to form a core of supporters. However, many may vote more as a sense of 'the best of a bad bunch' than because they actually like that party. Again the vote is a preference, but not a sign of support.

When models of voting behaviour seek to understand voting by discovering why a group of voters is attracted to or likes a particular party, they may be missing part of the story. The reasons why that group of people dislikes one of the other parties may be equally important. When there are only two options then the distinction is not crucial – dislike one then you must 'like' the other. But there are always at least three options. Even with only two parties standing there is always the alternative of not voting.

This mixing of support to mean both a vote and a sustained commitment occurs despite a recognition, and evidence, that the two are not the same thing. For example, 'comparing responses [to the party identification question] with the way in which people actually voted reveals that most people did not vote for the party to which they felt closest' (Dunleavy and Husbands, 1985, p.95). Similarly, Sarlvik and Crewe reported that in 1979 an eighth of voters had not voted for the party they identified with (1983, p.296), and Rose and McAllister suggest that 'a vote is not a 100 per cent endorsement of everything a party says or stands for. It is a rough indication of a preference, favouring one party as either a greater good or a lesser evil' (1986, p.8).

There seem to be three reasons for the unacknowledged acceptance of this underlying supposition that all votes are a sign of support, other than just following the lead of Butler and Stokes. They derive from ideas of democratic theory, the limitations of basic voting information and normal usage of the words 'support' and 'vote'. First, normative theories of democracy and representation presume that an election is used to find out what the electors want. For these theories to operate well, electors **should** express their wishes by voting for the candidate whose views best match their own. If there is a good match and therefore a 'sincere' vote, the choice is more than a preference, it is also a sign of blessing or 'support'. Second, the basic information we have when studying elections is the result of the choice not the reasons for it. So the motivation for choice that seems most used and believable is taken as applying to everyone in the absence of any means to distinguish between the bare marks on the ballot papers. Denver points out that voting and party identification are different – the latter is psychological and the former is behaviour, because you can see it. Party identification is ongoing, voting happens at specific times (Denver, 1989, p.27). But there is an assumption in the literature that the voting decision is determined by a certain psychological pattern: a like for the party. Authors fail to distinguish properly between the two levels. Third, those involved in politics (mainly politicians and the media) tend to use support as a synonym for vote. Such phrases as 'Can I count on your support?' are familiar in an election contest, and support as a synonym for vote is part of the normal election vocabulary. People are so used to the interchangeable nature of the terms 'vote' and 'support' in election campaigns that the orthodox assumption that a vote can be taken as a sign of support goes unquestioned.

'Rationality' of Voters

The third aspect of the orthodox interpretation to be considered is the idea of voters making rational decisions. Orthodox ideas about what should be studied also affect the importance of rationality, as those who are considered ill-informed are routinely ignored. While there is a distinct literature on 'rational voters', the idea of 'rationality' also has wider uses in voting behaviour studies. Four types of 'rationality' are apparent in the literature: the traditional 'economic' self-interest; a consistency of views; decisions based on 'objective facts' rather than emotions; and seeing the world in the same way as the analyst. Some of these views are expressly stated while others are apparent in the interpretational assumptions made by the different authors. All four types of rationality are considered here as part of the orthodox interpretation of voters. As with the previous two interpretational aspects, evidence of this assumption is shown and its effects are discussed.

Some disdain for ill-informed voters was evident in early voting behaviour material. The studies following the Columbia agenda found low levels of interest and few informed views on details of political life among their respondents. The Michigan school, therefore, looked for other factors to explain stability. Perhaps this is one excuse for the almost arrogant way in which voters' views that appeared 'irrational' or 'inconsistent' were ignored. Two examples from Butler and Stokes serve to illustrate this general approach in early works:

If we exclude from consideration those whose views wavered between inter-views and examine the inter-relationship of the attitudes only of those whose views remained fixed, we will be able to clear away most responses that had a random element and allow us to detect any patterns in the beliefs of the minority whose views were more genuine and stable. (1974, p.316)

And in the same vein: 'It seems more plausible to interpret the fluidity of the public's views as an indication of the limited degree to which attitudes are formed towards even the best-known of policy issues' (1974, p.281). This general approach seems to have continued, with psephologists often assuming that voters should think as the academics do. Even when attitudes and ideology are studied as the central explanation for the vote, some aspects of this approach continue.

Some writers assume a classic 'economic' rationality based upon self-interest and knowledge: 'Home owners anxious to keep their rates down would not be expected to favour Labour, identified as the party of high local rates' (Rose and McAllister, 1986, p.60). Similarly Heath's team suggest that:

it is not difficult to explain the difference in popularity. The universal benefits appeal to everyone's self-interest and they go to the salariat as much as, if not more than, to the working class. The selective benefits on the other hand go only to a minority, mainly the working class, and appeal to the altruism rather than the self-interest of the bulk of the electorate. (Heath et al., 1985, p.137)

Both of these quotes suggest voters are acting out of self-interest and know which party would most benefit them financially. The whole area of pocket-book and sociotropic voting, which looks at the link between perceived economic well-being and voting, follows these types of arguments (see, for example, Kinder and Kiewiet, 1981).

Assumptions that an individual will hold similar views on a range of issues are common. For example, Sarlvik and Crewe suggest that people with a conservative view on one thing will tend to have conservative views on others (1983, p.267). In constructing an attitude 'map', Heath's team decided that it was sufficient to use the responses to just one question to place voters on each axis (Heath *et al.*, 1985, p.118). They assumed that one question would provide a measure of each person's placement along an ideological continuum. In other words, they expect consistency of views on issues they see as similar.

A different strand relating to 'rationality' centres on the idea that a responsible voter should make a decision based on facts and that 'emotive' answers are not to be trusted. Here it is democratic theory that provides the reasoning, with the assumption that only informed citizens can make honest decisions at an election. Denver suggests that rising levels of education have enhanced the 'political sophistication' of voters and, as a result, emotionally-based attachments to political parties have declined in intensity (1989, p.49). Himmelweit's team suggest that 'there seems to be an implied pecking order in political science literature [of] how good citizens should form their judgements, a list of democratic desiderata for making vote choices. Issues are best, followed by the assessment of the candidate's or the leader's competence and integrity, with an evaluation of liking for them coming bottom of the list' (Himmelweit *et al.*, 1985, p.195).

Related to this desire for informed voters is an assumption about information levels. The non-emotive voter must make decisions based on good information. In this sense, the move from party-identification to issue-evaluation as the main explanation for voting behaviour is an evolutionary progression towards more rational voters. However, there is some recognition that 'some voters supported a party in the election despite, rather than because of, its policy in a particular area; others did not know what their chosen party stood for, sometimes they may well not have thought much about the matter before being asked about it in our interview' (Sarlvik and Crewe, 1983, p.206).

Perhaps the most prevalent facet of questioning the 'rationality' of voters is the general feeling that the analyst knows best. This may take the form of deciding the analyst knows better than the voters how they reached their decisions: 'People will not necessarily (and perhaps not often) articulate the influence of their social location in structuring their votes – the phenomenon may be objectively apparent to an analyst without being explicitly recognised by voters as involved in their decisions' (Dunleavy and Husbands, 1985, p.18). Even analysts from competing teams are assumed to have the correct views by Heath's team, who, when deciding which issues to use from past surveys, opted for those that the earlier researchers asked many or detailed questions on, because those were obviously the issues that the analysts had thought were important and so are the best ones to study (Heath *et al.*, 1991, p.42).

Others just presume to 'explain' the reasoning of voters: 'In general the public's feelings about immigration *must* be understood as a negative response to an unwanted societal change rather than as a reaction to actual contacts with the immigrant population' [emphasis added] (Sarlvik and Crewe, 1983, p.242). Similarly, Heath's team argue that 'It is in our view *more plausible to suppose* that it was people's experiences of the winter of discontent in 1979 that led them to take a rather gloomy view of their own real incomes' [emphasis added] (Heath *et al.*, 1991, p.150). Others assume that voters share the analysts' own 'objective' recognition of the true position, or assume they should see the world in the way political scientists or academics do: 'there are grounds for thinking that Labour actually moved to the left between 1970 and 1974, but that the electorate failed to notice, or perhaps believe, the shift' (Heath *et al.*, 1985, p.146) or 'as we have seen, individual voters' opinions are not necessarily constrained by any sharp ideological demarcation lines between the parties' (Sarlvik and Crewe, 1983, p.180).

Sometimes the authors seem unwilling to believe the voters so that 'the reasons that electors offer for their vote need not be taken at their face value' (Rose and McAllister, 1986, p.127). Others are condescending in their acceptance of voters' views: 'voters have displayed a fair amount of rationality and sophistication' (Heath *et al.*, 1991, p.44) or 'the majority of voters changed for *good reasons*' [emphasis added] (Himmelweit *et al.*, 1985, p.40). Sarlvik and Crewe question 'the extent to which voters hold *realistic views* of the meaning of the choice alternatives' [emphasis added] (1983, p.202) and decry respondents who think differently: 'as always with survey questions, small proportions of voters ... clearly have "*got it wrong*"' [emphasis added] (1983, p.186).

However, various authors do on occasion recognize that a difference between the 'rationality' of voters and psephologists is not unexpected. As Rose and McAllister point out, 'It would be extraordinary if the median British voter, a working-class person leaving school at 15, thought about voting the same way as a middle-class PhD in public choice economics' (1986, p.126). There is also some recognition that voters do not always have the information that political scientists possess. For instance, Dunleavy and Husbands point out that in 1983 not all voters would know if they were in a marginal seat because there had been boundary changes and not all voters have access to *The BBC/ITN Guide to the New Parliamentary Constituencies*, as the analysts did (1985, p.189). Of course, not only would many voters not have access to this work, but they would also not know of its existence or necessarily have an interest in consulting it. The authors assume that voters would normally know if they lived in a marginal seat and it is only the redrawing of the boundaries that may have confused them. Such an assumption is asking a lot of the average voter, especially as commentators themselves rarely agree on which seats are marginal.

The effects of assuming rationality

When rational behaviour is either expected or deemed necessary, any other behaviour is overlooked. So, if analysts believe that voters will vote tactically by moving from the third-placed to the second-placed party, that is the only type of tactical voting that is measured. Similarly, only those who have views that seem internally consistent and relate to the party voted for are deemed to be 'rational' issue voters, despite the literature showing that few actually think like that (for example, Scarbrough, 1984). In various places the self-perception of the voter is said to be important, but more often, the interpretation of the writer is taken as applying in general.

Despite a desire for consistency, the authors also face problems when trying to define views on some issues in ideological terms. Throughout the studies there are certain issues that present particular enigmas. Britain's position in relation to the EEC (now the European Union) is a prime example. Labour and the Conservatives have both changed their position regarding British membership of the European Union. Such changes provide problems for the labelling of attitudes:

It [pro-EEC view] was coded in a 'Conservative' direction following that party's policy in the 1970s in favour of joining the EEC. Yet it was only in 1974, after Britain's entry, that it fell within the Conservative space [on the cognitive map]. In 1970 it was closer to the 'Labour' cluster, reflecting the fact that it was a *Labour* Government ... which had tried hard to bring Britain into the EEC. (Himmelweit *et al.*, 1985, p.143)

An arbitrary definition of the 'liberal' view on the Common Market is even admitted by Heath *et al.* (1985, p.65). When the parties and analysts cannot decide which attitude towards the EEC matches the Conservative or Labour view, what chance does the voter have?

Assumptions of 'perfect' information, which usually means the kind of understanding and assessment that a political scientist would make, cause problems. Of particular note is the way a 'lack' of information is treated. A good example is the way in which the fact that few can correctly name their own MP is taken as a sign of political naivety. Perhaps such a finding should instead be taken as a sign that local MPs are not vitally important to most voters and so there is no need for voters to know their MP's name. In many countries using alternative voting systems, where the British obsession with a constituency MP is not a feature, few would be expected to know the name of a local representative.

In assuming some sort of rationality on the part of voters when they choose the best option, the orthodox approach drastically reduces the number of voters it will consider. When all voters who behave in a way that is deemed to be not rational in some way are excluded or ignored, a vast amount of real behaviour is left unexplained by models working within the orthodox interpretation and parameters. Add to this scrapheap those voters who do not see an election as a time to choose the best option and those who do not feel a strong commitment to the party for which they voted, and the detrimental effects of the orthodox interpretation increase.

System Biases

The fourth part of the orthodoxy to be discussed in this chapter relates to ideas about the factors that can be ignored in the study of voting behaviour. As described in Chapter 1, the orthodoxy concentrates on general trends in the behaviour of major party voters. As a consequence, local context and details specific to the election in each area are not covered. In particular, system biases such as the effect of the electoral and party systems are not mentioned. This enduring habit of studying a two-party system and the lack of comment on the effect of the voting system are now discussed.

In much of the early voting behaviour literature a two-party system is taken for granted and the decision to concentrate on Labour and the Conservatives is not mentioned. Studies that look at elections post-1983 tend to mention the Liberals (in one of their manifestations) and talk, to some extent, of a multi-party system. However, the other 'third' parties that have MPs, namely the

Scottish and Welsh nationalists (SNP and Plaid Cymru), are systematically ignored. There is an almost unanimous agreement about a
two-party system in earlier decades, despite the existence of some
Liberal MPs after every election as well as the periodic presence of
Nationalist MPs. For example, Sarlvik and Crewe suggest that 1979
saw the return to a two-party system that had been there from
1945 to 1970 (1983, p.5), while Denver talks of the dominance of
the two-party system in the period 1950–70 (1989, pp.120–1).
Heath's team differ in their watershed, talking of 1983 as a remarkable
election, with the success of the Liberal–SDP Alliance signalling the
end of the two-party dominance of the post-war period (Heath *et al.*,
1985, p.1).

In the early works no mention is made of the acceptance of
a two-party system, although such an assumption is clear, with
survey questions systematically asking for views on only Labour
and Conservative policies, performance or leaders (for example
Butler and Stokes, 1974, p.452; Sarlvik and Crewe, 1983, p.186).
The later studies do generally include the Liberals or Alliance in
their questions (for example Dunleavy and Husbands, 1985, p.102;
Heath *et al.*, 1985, p.97). However, the reported analyses often
concentrate on the two major parties, as the following examples
illustrate: a table looking at 'right wing' agreement looks only at
Conservative and Labour voters (Heath *et al.*, 1985, p.111); when
looking at positive and negative comments on the Conservatives
and Labour on various issues no mention is made of other parties
(Sarlvik and Crewe, 1983, p.134); tables in the chapters on popular
capitalism and pocket-book voting look at Conservative, Labour and
'other' voters (Heath *et al.*, 1991, Chapters 8 and 9). Studies of the
1983 and 1987 elections do generally include mention of the
Alliance and attitudes towards the party and its leaders.

Many of the techniques that are habitually used to analyse voting
behaviour in Britain are dependent on a two-party system. One of
the most obvious examples is the neat two-class, two-party model
and the different ways in which its strength is measured. Both the
Alford index and odds ratios can only be calculated for a pair of
parties and classes (see section in Chapter 4) although Heath and
colleagues do say that they could calculate the Liberal figure
too, against each of the other parties (Heath *et al.*, 1985, p.31)
(but they do not show them). Swing also works best and most
intuitively when there are only two options (see section in Chapter 3).
Other approaches do not escape either, with many attitude variables

being presented as having a 'Conservative' versus 'Labour' polarity. Axes, by definition, have only two ends, so the use of such scales to present attitude placement also militates against a multi-polar approach. The very centrality of the left–right scale in political rhetoric suggests polarity on one divide only, giving just two distinct positions. Similarly, many numerical statistical techniques work best with a dichotomous dependent variable, such as tree-analysis, logit or linear regression. These techniques need to divide people in the dataset into just two groups that are then compared, so using such processes means that categories have to be simplified into two *blocs*.

As Butler and Stokes honestly point out, you do not need to treat all variables as dichotomies, but it is easier to do so (1974, p.294). However, when the rise of third parties became too great to ignore, conflict arose between the political situation and the customary approach. A variety of measures have been adopted to retain dichotomous techniques with a three-party system, such as exile, inclusion and continuums, as the three following examples illustrate. Butler and Stokes exile the Liberals by using a basic two-class, two-party table and mentioning in a footnote that this is rather a simplification (1974, p.74). Heath and colleagues include the Liberals with the Conservatives as middle-class (Heath *et al.*, 1991, pp.64–5). Sarlvik and Crewe use a continuum of ideological voting with the Liberals in the middle (1983, p.288). In each case the writers are attempting to squeeze the third party into the two-party framework.

First-past-the-post has a strong effect on the real choice given to voters, as 'voters can only choose in response to the alternatives put before them by the parties'(Rose and McAllister, 1986, p.4). The latter authors discuss the effect of the voting system further, noting that 'the translation of voters' preferences into representatives in the House of Commons depends not only upon how individuals vote, but also upon where they vote and the ranking of parties in their constituency' (p.4). However, this attention to the effects of the electoral system is unusual, perhaps related to the fact that Ian McAllister has lived in Australia, which uses other electoral systems, for some time. More typically, Sarlvik and Crewe ask what might have happened under a different system (1983, pp.289–90), but do not mention the possible effects of the first-past-the-post electoral system in other parts of their discussion. Similarly, when they comment that many people no longer accept the choice of just the two major parties there is no mention of the effect of the electoral system (p.281). The studies concentrate on how and why the vote is cast for a particular party, but pay scant attention to the way in which this mass decision is translated into MPs in the House of Commons. For instance, little is made of the fact that in February 1974 the Conservatives won the most votes but did not form the government, or that the second Thatcher victory in 1983, while giving the party a bigger majority in the House, was won on a lower level of votes.

While Crewe and Norris argue that 'The impact of the electoral system (strictly speaking, the part of it that defined the aggregation of votes and the criterion for winning) has always been on the agenda' (1992, p.19), it does not seem to have been on the voting behaviour agenda. There is a burgeoning literature on the effects of electoral systems on other aspects of the political system, but it has remained separated from the voting behaviour literature. Of the books covered in this study only three (Rose and McAllister, 1986; Himmelweit *et al.*, 1985; Sarlvik and Crewe, 1983) list the electoral system in the index. These and other writers do mention the electoral system, but often just in passing. Rarely are the implications of the first-past-the-post electoral system spelt out.

The political parties are affected by the first-past-the-post electoral system. The effect on the Liberals is fairly frequently commented upon (for example Himmelweit *et al.*, 1985, pp.162, 172, 179; Heath *et al.*, 1985, p.3; Heath *et al.*, 1991, p.24; Rose and McAllister, 1986, p.23). The common view is that '... some proportion of the voters in "the middle ground" will be discouraged from voting Liberal for fear of wasting their votes and thus assisting the party they liked least to come to power' (Sarlvik and Crewe, 1983, p.289). But the effects of the system are just as likely to be ignored by analysts even when the workings of the electoral system have some bearing on the area being discussed. For example, when Heath *et al.* discuss the fact that the Alliance was not able to secure the votes of most of its potential voters they do not mention the probable effect of the electoral system (1985, p.123).

Discussion of the effect of the system on the major parties is even more rare, though there are a few exceptions. Sarlvik and Crewe note that the first-past-the-post system 'has all but ensured that one of the two larger parties achieves a parliamentary majority ... The election system thus has the double effect of helping the Conservatives and Labour to hold on to their voting support in the middle ground and of focusing attention at election time on the choice between government by the Conservatives or government by Labour' (1983, p.289). Heath's team also comment that the 'division of Britain into two political nations [has] also had important consequences for the operation of the electoral system. In particular it means that Labour's loss of votes has not been reflected in the number of seats that it holds in the House of Commons' (Heath *et al.*, 1985, p.74). Himmelweit's team suggest that 'the reasons for the changing fortunes of an almost identical share of the votes have to do with the vagaries of the British electoral system. An election in Britain is won not on the basis of which party obtains the largest share of the votes but, because of the First-Past-the-Post system, by the relative distribution of votes within each constituency' (Himmelweit *et al.*, 1985, p.32). Rose and McAllister note that 'the electoral system restricts seats in the House of Commons to parties capable of concentrating their support in some constituencies' (1986, p.16). However, none of the authors look in great detail at the effects of the electoral system or build such effects into the overall model of voting behaviour.

Effects of ignoring system biases

Much of the way in which voting behaviour is studied depends on the existing first-past-the-post electoral system and a predominant two-party system. It may be valid to argue that those are what we do or did have (although a two-party system is now difficult to defend across all of Britain) and that they therefore understandably moulded ideas. Nevertheless, some recognition of the constraints imposed by these system aspects would be useful. The first-past-the-post electoral system affects the parties and so affects the choice offered to voters and so affects the voting decision. Consideration of the working of the electoral system would therefore seem a vital component of the study of voting behaviour. A tie between the electoral system and prevalent party system is discussed in other areas of political studies. Duverger's hypothesis is that a plurality system tends towards two parties and a proportional system tends towards multiple parties (Duverger, 1986).

The two-party system structures the choices that voters face and so influences their voting decision. There was some recognition of the importance of parties in structuring the voting decisions:

The role played by the parties in giving shape and direction to the behaviour of voters is so taken for granted that its importance is easily missed.

Without it, however, the mass of the people could scarcely participate in regular transfers of power. Individual electors accept the parties as leading actors on the political stage and see in partisan terms the meaning of the choices which the universal franchise puts before them. (Butler and Stokes, 1974, p.19)

And some recognition that choice is restricted by what is actually on offer: 'Obviously, with at most three or four parties to choose from – many would probably count only the two major parties as real alternatives – voting decisions have to be based on judgements about which of the parties is closest to one's own views rather than a matter of looking for a perfect match' (Sarlvik and Crewe, 1983, p.248).

Importantly, in terms of the study of voting behaviour, the workings of the electoral system restrict some of the decisions that are made. If these decisions are taken for granted then what is studied and how it is studied will also be affected. Many may expect voters to vote for their favourite, but first-past-the-post may lead to a tactical vote and 'thus our knowledge of what voters want is limited to those choices which the existing voting system allows them to express' (Dunleavy, 1990, p.462). More importantly, in view of earlier arguments about the different decisions a voter may make, the first-past-the-post electoral system enforces a situation of preferring only one party. A voter marks a single cross on the paper whether the party is 'the least worst on offer' or an embodiment of the voter's world view.

This point brings us back full circle to the problems of assuming that all voters choose the 'best' party. The aspects of the voting behaviour orthodoxy relating to ideas of what is to be studied are clearly interrelated with orthodox views on how key components are interpreted. Only studying major party voters and well informed voters makes it easier to assume that voters make informed decisions about the best option. Similarly, in leaving aside consideration of the effect of the electoral system, questions about decisions other than which party is best are not raised. Voters who are not choosing the best option and are not in full agreement with the policies of the party for which they vote, and who make the decision for reasons that are not accepted by the analysts will not be included in the orthodox models of voting behaviour. The next section examines three recognized types of voting behaviour which fit this description.

Consequences of the Orthodox Concepts

Consideration of negatively motivated voting, a protest vote and tactical voting will illustrate problems with the orthodox interpretation of voting behaviour. All three types of behaviour have been written about, within the core voting behaviour literature as well as in more specific texts. Although all of the core models are based on the assumption that the important decision to explain is in terms of which party is best liked, other types of voting decision are mentioned. Several refer to tactical voting (for example Johnston *et al.*, 1988, p.64; Heath *et al.*, 1991, pp.52–60; Himmelweit *et al.*, 1985, p.177) or allude to a tactical situation (Dunleavy and Husbands, 1985, p.198). Other decision types mentioned relate to rejection, so that 'Voters can pass judgement on the government and either keep it in office or replace it' (Denver, 1989, p.3). Some ask if floating voters' votes are 'more often a vote against their former party than a vote for the party to which they turn?' (Himmelweit *et al.*, 1985, p.40). Negative voting is also mentioned (for example Dunleavy and Husbands, 1985, p.214; Rose and McAllister, 1986, p.52), while Sarlvik and Crewe consider negative partisanship (1983, pp.301–3). Another type of negatively motivated vote is a protest vote, designed to send a signal to the party normally voted for. Heath *et al.* have a subsection on the protest vote (1985, pp.121–3) and many others mention it, although usually in relation to the Liberals (for example Himmelweit *et al.*, 1985, p.37; Sarlvik and Crewe, 1983, p.298; Heath *et al.*, 1985, pp.7 and 113).

Although tactical, negative and protest voting are mentioned in the orthodox texts, they are not thoroughly analysed, and evidence for their existence is not well documented. So, besides considering how the orthodoxy hinders the full study of these types of behaviour and what has been written about them, it is also important to note the ways in which the orthodox concepts impinge upon their study. In examining these three types of behaviour the conceptual barriers created by the orthodox approach will be illustrated.

Negative motivations

At the most basic, a negative motivation will result in a negative vote. For example, Jo votes Labour because she hates the Conservatives. In its simplest form, a negative vote is one cast for a party because that party is not another, strongly disliked, party.

A negative voter may well like the party voted for, but what makes it a negative vote is that the dislike is stronger than the like: although Jo likes Labour the intensity of her hatred for the Conservatives is greater. There are also other aspects and connotations of a more general negative motivation that are important in assessing overall voting behaviour. Most prominent is the separate literature on retrospective judgements (see Fiorina, 1981) and voting as punishment rather than reward. Negative motivations have also been looked at in connection with positive views, such as the use of combined measures of negative and positive partisanship to find the 'hard core supporters' (Sarlvik and Crewe, 1983, p.305). When there are a range of options and the voter has to choose just one, feelings against some options are likely to play a part along with feelings in favour of other options.

The different assumptions examined in the previous sections of this chapter combine to marginalize a study of negative motivations in the vote. Most obviously, both the idea that a vote is a sign of support and the idea that the vote decision is about which party is best, ignore the possibility of a negatively motivated vote. The electoral system is also set up to suggest that the vote is a sign of support and so does not recognize a negative vote. The common ideas about what constitutes a rational vote also emphasize the choosing of the best, although there is some acceptance that the 'best' might be the 'least worst'. Another connotation of 'rational' voting also militates against the widespread study of negative voting: the suggestion that a negative vote is somehow emotive rather than based on facts. Acceptance of the two-party system without comment means that negative motivation can be ignored, because with only two choices, one will be liked and the other disliked, so why not just study the liked.

A voting choice is the result of a decision about the different options on offer made after consideration of a variety of relevant criteria. Many studies in the field of social psychology have considered aspects of evaluation. The most widely accepted model used to explain the way in which a view is reached is the 'weighted average model' (Baron and Byrne, 1984, p.114), which proposes that each relevant piece of information is given a weight and then the total is averaged. The way is which different types of information are weighted is of particular interest in the discussion of negative voting. Specifically, Fiske concluded that: 'Considerable evidence shows that negatively valanced [directioned] information receives more weight than positive information' (1980, p.891). Her research also found that an overall impression of a person is more heavily influenced by extreme than by normal aspects. Although Fiske was working on how impressions of people are affected, other work has applied the weighted average model to attitudes, groups and beliefs (Fiske, 1980, p.892). Applying these findings to the vote choice seems to suggest that one strong negative view could outweigh several mild positive ones, making negative voting an important motivation.

Elections in the early 1990s in Britain, the United States and Australia saw the extensive use of negative campaigning. Voters in the USA were warned that a vote for the other party would result in higher taxes, and in Australia the scare was of new taxes. In the British 1992 election the Conservatives warned that Labour would increase taxes and inflation, while Labour raised the spectre of increased unemployment and a declining welfare state if the Conservatives won. In each case the dire consequences of a victory for the other side were emphasized rather than the beneficial results of a win by the party making the appeal. This emphasis on negative campaigning is not new, but seems to be growing in profile. If campaigning is going to rest increasingly on scare tactics and negative campaigning, then the study of negative aspects of the voting decision assume crucial importance. While parties are campaigning to persuade voters primarily not to vote for the opposition, voting studies cannot realistically continue to concentrate on why voters did vote for their party with no study of why they did not vote for the other parties.

A negative motivation may be the primary reason for the vote, it may form an important part of the overall assessment of the options or it may help to reinforce a long-standing identification with a party. To look fully at the part played by negative views, consideration must be given to relative measures of feeling and to views on the parties that were not voted for as well as the one that was. Using information on how each voter feels about the whole range of parties facilitates the identification of voters whose strongest feeling is negative (or positive) and those who have negative feelings towards most of the parties. The use of this type of information necessitates the setting aside of some parts of the voting behaviour orthodoxy.

A protest vote

Iqbal usually votes Labour, but disagrees with their recent policy document on transport and is cross with the way several senior party members have been behaving recently, so he decides to vote for another party. This is an example of a protest vote, when a voter who normally votes for one party chooses at an election to vote for a different party in response to some disliked action of the normal party. The party that is normally voted for is the intended recipient of the voting message, not the party given the vote. It is similar to a consumer boycott.

Both the orthodox assumptions that a vote is a sign of support and that voters decide on the best party exclude ideas of a protest vote. A rational voter would not cast a protest vote, because one vote is not that important and the deserted party cannot receive the message. For a protest vote to be measured by aggregate or survey data, it has to be cast in a way that the analysts recognize – so that they think it is rational. This means deserting the party that is popularly seen as having upset its voters and casting the vote for an acceptable receptacle of protest, such as a third party. In a two-party system a protest vote is difficult, as the only option for protest is the other major party (the Opposition) and so may be unpalatable. The other alternative is to abstain, which is usually not measured in studies of voting.

A protest vote is a classic example of an action where the motivation rather than the act must be measured. When behaviour at a single election is considered and all votes are taken as a sign of support, a protest vote is invisible. Even when information on two subsequent elections is considered a protest may still fail to stand out. All that would show, if data on how individuals voted at each election are used, is a movement from one party to another. To discover if the vote is a protest, a conversion or something else, the voter must be asked the reasons for the switch. When information about voters' longer voting history is gathered a protest vote has more chance of showing, as it should be the one different vote in a series of votes for the same party. However, the motivation of the voters still needs to be checked, as that blip may actually have been a short-lived conversion – a single-issue vote – or it may have been motivated by the personality of the local candidates. When voting is studied at the aggregate level by looking at the number or percentage of votes received by each candidate or party, protest voting has no chance of being identified. With gross measures, only the large, widespread changes show, as smaller ones can be cancelled out by switches in the opposite direction (see Chapter 3).

A protest vote may seem like an irrational act: giving a party normally opposed a vote because of some displeasure with the party usually liked. However, the level at which voters aim their vote is important in understanding a protest vote. The casting of a vote could have three possible sources: the national scene and overall standing of the party; the constituency contest; an action that the voter must live with. While a protest vote seems to be an action aimed at the party normally voted for, the personal level may be more important. A vote is secret to all except the person casting it, and the voter must live with that action. If the voter found the voting decision easy and has strong feelings for the party given the vote, then living with the vote will not be a problem.

However, a vote cast with more uncertainty or with less clearly self-perceived motivation may raise psychological qualms. When an action is at odds with normally held attitudes, the individual may experience an uneasy feeling that social psychologists call dissonance (Baron and Byrne, 1984, p.115). When dissonance occurs, the individual will try to reduce it by removing the lack of fit between attitude and action. But, in the case of a vote, the action cannot be changed, so either the views or the perception of the action must shift. If the individual concerned has a good reason for the action, dissonance is minimal (Baron and Byrne, 1984, p.156). While the specific studies conducted by social psychologists in this area may not have a direct bearing on the voting decision, the issues raised do pose some interesting questions. If we accept that a vote has a strong psychological component, being an action voters must live with, then it is important to look at the rationalization offered by the voter.

A protest vote may not alter the election result, but it is important for the voter and so should be seriously studied. In the orthodoxy, the aim of voting behaviour analysts is to study the different levels of the vote received by each party. If this is the only aim, then all voting behaviour that does not alter the fortunes of the parties, such as a protest vote, will be ignored. Even if so many voters protested in the same way that the effect on the parties was noticeable, such behaviour would still be ignored by the orthodox interpretation because those voters are not choosing the best party. However, those voters are making a considered decision based on strong political views. To the protest voter, the act of denying a party one vote is important. To understand fully the behaviour of voters, it is vital to consider such behaviour as protest voting, which has a personal motivation but little effect on the overall election result.

Tactical voting

Heather likes the Green party best, thinks the Liberal Democrats are pretty good and is neutral about the Conservatives. She also detests Labour, but thinks the Labour candidate will win in her constituency. Heather votes Liberal Democrat, as she thinks they have the best chance of beating the Labour candidate. Heather casts a tactical vote. A tactical vote is cast for a party that is your second (or third or fourth) preference, because you think they have the best chance of defeating a strongly disliked party.

This phenomenon is perhaps the best example of how the conceptual assumptions in the voting behaviour orthodoxy act to exclude a type of voting behaviour. A tactical vote does not fit with either the idea that a vote is a sign of support or the idea that voters decide on the best party. Downs (1957, pp.47–9) does say that a tactical vote may be rational, but only when there are more than two options. Here, the normal assumption of a two-party system has worked against serious consideration of tactical voting. When a three-party situation is accepted and tactical voting talked of, the third party is usually assumed to be the recipient of such votes, perhaps because their arrival on the scene created the possibility. Under the first-past-the-post system, a tactical vote is a real alternative for many voters, as it is seen as the only way to work the system. But the fact that all a voter can do is place an 'X' against one name makes such a vote impossible to detect in voting data. Most studies that do try to measure tactical voting fall into the 'perfect information' and 'rationality' problems. This trait is true of approaches using both surveys and data on votes cast.

Tactical voting is usually measured by looking at the changes in the percentage of the vote received by the second- and third-placed parties in marginal constituencies. So if the vote for the third-placed party drops by 1,000 votes and the second-placed party gains that number, it is assumed that tactical voting was the reason. Aggregate measures of tactical voting, like similar measures of volatility, gauge net rather than gross levels and so miss some categories of tactical voters (Catt, 1990, p.18). For instance, tactical voters switching from the fourth- to third-placed party would not be detected. When analysts are deciding which moves can be decoded as tactical, they usually assume that voters will know that they are in a constituency where a tactical vote would be 'sensible'. That is, a constituency where the party they dislike is likely to win and where their favourite party will not be second, and where the marginality suggests the possibility of the incumbent losing. So only tactical voters with 'perfect information' in a relevant seat will be counted. Looking only at voters who have switched parties also excludes those who voted tactically the last time. Regular tactical voters will show as consistent voters rather than switchers.

Again we have the problem of whether it is the motive or the resulting action and its possible effect that are important. Is a tactical vote a vote cast with tactical considerations in mind, regardless of how misplaced the reading of the situation, or is a tactical vote one that can be seen as a 'sensible' switch? Detecting potential or actual tactical voting with surveys is difficult because of the complexity of the necessary questions and problems of respondents recognizing or admitting to that type of activity. The exact question used can affect the result to a great extent (Catt, 1989, p.551).

However, if a tactical vote is taken as the convergence of three separate attitudes (Catt, 1990), then its measurement in surveys would become easier. The three necessary attitudes are: a great dislike of one party, leading to a paramount desire to see them defeated; a desire to cast a strategic vote (one that will affect the result); and a willingness to gather information on the best way of casting an effective vote. Each of these attitudes can be measured separately and thus the different combinations separated. Much of the behaviour that is presently counted as tactical would be strategic rather than tactical in the above model.

Following the 1987 general election, in which tactical voting was widely discussed, there were a series of attempts to measure its extent. Some looked at aggregate measures across the country (Galbraith and Rae, 1989; Johnston and Pattie, 1991) or ascertained the effect on the size of each party in parliament (Curtice and Steed, 1988), while others utilized survey data (Heath et al., 1991; Niemi et al., 1992). Disagreement over the extent of tactical voting resulted in a range from 6.5 per cent (Heath et al., 1991, p.54) to 'about one in every six voters [17%]' (Niemi et al., 1992, p.229). Arguments about the different measures and their validity are heated, but what none of the authors is refuting is the existence of tactical voters. Heath's team comment on the low levels of tactical voting, but even taking their measure of 6.5 per cent, this relates to 2,114,412 voters. About two million voters may still be seen as not many when compared to the total electorate, but it equates to 32 average-sized constituencies, almost four times the combined Nationalist vote or more than the total number of votes cast in an election in New Zealand. All of these groups have been individually studied, which would refute claims that the group is too small to be worth analysis. If tactical voting does exist, then it needs to be understood and that explanation cannot be part of the orthodox interpretation based on explaining why voters like a given party.

There are problems with the measurement of tactical voting, but that does not mean it can be ignored. Neither do findings suggesting that few behave in this way justify its neglect. To understand fully the complexities and implications of a tactical vote and therefore to pick up all instances of it, some of the aspects of the voting behaviour orthodoxy must be set aside. There is also the question of measuring potential tactical voters who do not live in a relevant constituency as well as those who do. If the aim of the study of voting behaviour is to understand the way in which voters behave, rather than to explain any given election result, then all aspects of tactical voting must be considered.

Summary

In the orthodox interpretation it is assumed that voters choose 'the best option' and therefore a vote can be decoded as a sign of support. However, voters may be making other decisions and so are indicating a preference rather than showing a desire to sustain their party. A tactical vote is a good example of one that indicates preference in the context rather than support, and which was motivated by dislike and a desire to affect the result rather than the choice of the best party. In concentrating on just one type of decision, the orthodox approach ignores other types of choices that are made by voters. Assumptions of some sort of rational behaviour on the part of voters also permeate the voting behaviour literature. Different types of 'rationality' are stressed by different authors, but together, the range of ways in which rationality is expected hide some sorts of voting decisions. The fourth aspect of the orthodoxy to be considered was the absence of discussion of the ways in which the choices that are made at election time are affected by both the party system

and the electoral system. By neglecting such system biases, important factors in the overall equation are lost, thus diminishing the
total picture.

The orthodox approach concentrates on general trends and
mainstream behaviour. Voters who decide which party they like
best and vote for it as a sign of commitment are covered by the
orthodoxy. Anyone who sees the voting decision in another way is
excluded. Voters who prefer the party but are not committed to it,
are not recognized. The orthodox interpretations of the vote restrict
the range of voting behaviour that is studied and misrepresent the
actions of some voters. The way in which the political situation
moulds the election choice is also ignored. In short, the problem
with the orthodox approach is that it limits the study of voting
behaviour to a study of the typical voter.

3

Data Collection, Aggregation and Analysis

Data are vital to the study of voting behaviour and their use is as much a part of the orthodoxy as are interpretation and concepts. As outlined in Chapter 1, there are three key aspects to the methodological part of the orthodoxy. Data are collected using nationwide surveys, with an emphasis on ensuring continuity in the measures used. These data are then aggregated to study groups and general trends, rather than individuals. Finally, analysis tends towards powerful statistical techniques in an effort to explain why each party received the votes it did. These methodological aspects of the orthodoxy will be considered to reveal the limitations they place on our understanding of voting behaviour in Britain.

Voting behaviour studies look at the actions of voters and try to describe, explain or understand them. To do this requires information on the behaviour of voters, and there are only two sources of such information. Researchers can either ask people what they did and what they think or they can look at the official recording of the actions of voters published as the total number of votes cast in each constituency. Census data provide a hybrid data source, as individuals are asked to respond to questions about themselves, but the results are published in an aggregated form. Therefore, voting behaviour studies rely upon survey responses or official, aggregated statistics. While these are the only possible sources of information on voting behaviour, they are not without their limitations.

Problems with the use of surveys and aggregate measures are considered in the first two sections of this chapter. Work from a range of academics who have studied these problems is used to show some of the shortcomings of the orthodox methodology. These criticisms are not new, but they are neither mentioned in nor borne in mind by the mainstream voting behaviour texts. In the last section, two specific areas that are affected by the methodological orthodoxy are examined. Looking at groups of voters who are routinely excluded from analysis illustrates the limitations of the methods, and finally, the frequently used measure of swing is used as a case study to show the effects of the methodological parts of the orthodoxy. While these topics associated with methods are, by definition, related to statistics, the arguments considered here do not involve lots of arithmetic, equations or Greek symbols. Most of the underlying questions and criticisms relate to concepts and processes rather than to numerically based arguments.

Problems of Survey Data

In Britain, like the USA, one series of election surveys is central to voting behaviour studies. While three different teams have now had control of the British Election Series (BES), there are certain aspects central to all of these. Each was carried out after the election and questioned a sample of people across Great Britain (south of the Caledonian Canal) using face-to-face interviews. For each, there was a panel element where some of the people interviewed in the previous survey were re-interviewed to give measures of change in views and behaviour. In all of the surveys, questions are predominantly of the type where the responses are suggested (forced-response questions), and there is an emphasis on continuity of questions across the series. Studies conducted outside of this series have also been based on face-to-face interviews using mostly forced-response questions. Some of the criticisms of this method of data collection are specific to the way in which the British surveys, especially the central series, have been conducted, but others relate to all surveys. Because surveys provide the basic information used to study voting behaviour, it is important to consider if they have any limitations, and the possible effects these may have on the analysis of voting behaviour.

Surveys in general

A survey depends upon the replies to set questions, so the wording of such questions is vitally important: ask a bad question and you may receive unusable replies. While many of the rules for good question wording are common sense, such as keeping it simple and readable, other aspects are less obvious or intuitive. Criticisms of surveys in general relate mainly to the problems of recording the opinions, attitudes or beliefs of individuals accurately, and of recognizing the shortcomings inherent in the process. Typically, two kinds of information are acquired through surveys: attitudes and facts. Attitude questions range widely and can cover a spectrum from specific issues to general perceptions. The facts collected in voting behaviour surveys usually relate to the casting of the vote and to demographic variables such as gender, age, class and occupation. All rely both on the respondents reporting what they think or do accurately and honestly and on the reliable codification of such information.

There are limits to what types of factual information can be gathered using surveys. Some questions of fact are difficult to measure in surveys, due to limitations of memory (parent's occupation when young), not having the detailed information (net family annual income) or uncertainty over category differences (highest educational qualification). Schreiber (1975, pp.499 and 505) found some evidence that ascribed characteristics, such as gender or race, are more reliably reported than are achieved ones, such as education or occupation. This difference may be due to uncertainty about the possible response categories and what they mean or the problems of always gaining enough information from respondents to be able to code accurately variables such as occupation. Voting behaviour surveys routinely collect factual data on an individual's background, but make little mention of possible measurement problems.

Most criticisms of survey data relate to the measurement of attitudes. While opinion surveys are widely used in the social sciences, the study of them as a tool is patchy. Important issues are raised in some of the studies that have been done on the use of this tool. Such questions need to be addressed in any area that depends heavily on opinion survey data. Some critics of such data argue that no set question can properly measure the richness of real views or be understood by all (Singer, 1988). However, these general complaints are not addressed here. Instead, detailed limitations on the conduct of good surveys are examined. While all voting behaviour studies utilize data gathered from surveys, they do not discuss the limitations of this method or the effects these may have on the result.

Various studies have shown that certain changes to the way in which a question is worded can alter the responses. Schuman and Presser (1981), by experimentation, found that respondents were more likely to report strong feeling for an issue than that it was important in their decision to vote (p.249), and that small word changes such as 'forbid' rather than 'not allow' can significantly alter results (p.296). Hippler and Schwarz (1986) tested the 'forbid' versus 'not allow' difference and suggested that the variation is due to 'indifferents' not wishing to endorse the proposition, whether it be to 'forbid' or 'allow', thus boosting the 'not' part of the reply. Smith (1987) showed more negative responses to 'welfare' than 'poor', and unearthed hidden connotations of waste associated with the former. Studies such as these concentrate on the effect of details of the question and sometimes show only small differences that some may see as not worth bothering about. The problem is that we do not know what effect some changes in the wording of a question will have: 'The basic problem is not that every wording change shifts proportions – far from it – but that it is extraordinarily difficult to know in advance which changes will alter marginals [percentage giving each response] and which will not' (Schuman and Presser, 1981, p.312). Set questions, as used in surveys, may contain words that will bias the replies.

Other wording changes may alter the way in which replies can be interpreted. One good example is whether or not a 'don't know' or 'can't say' option is offered as a possible answer. Respondents tend to try to work within the framework provided, so are less likely to say 'don't know' if it is not explicitly offered (Schuman and Presser, 1981, p.299; Bishop et al., 1986). While omission of a 'don't know' category will increase the number expressing a view, the proportions choosing each of the other options tend to remain the same. This finding suggests that where those who would otherwise choose 'don't know' are forced to make a choice, they are representative of the population in their views. Therefore a 'don't know' option should be included if an 'informed opinion' on the issue is wanted, but can be omitted if what is wanted are basic values or general attitudes (Schuman and Presser, 1981, p.312). While the Butler and Stokes (1974, Appendix B) survey does include a suggestion of a 'don't know' response in every relevant question, neither the 1979 nor the 1987 survey does, although it is indicated to the interviewee that such a response is acceptable (Heath et al., 1991, pp.250–309). Hippler and Schwarz (1986) go further and suggest that 'don't know' is not always the relevant alternative and perhaps 'don't care' would be better, as people may know that what they feel is indifference. While the provision or not of a 'don't know' option can alter the marginals, reports on levels of responses rarely specify whether or not such an option was provided or how many used it.

Other changes in the range of responses offered to respondents can also have an effect. Schuman (1986, p.436) reports on an experiment on this aspect of question wording. He asked respondents what was the 'most important issue' facing the country and provided a choice of four issue options, plus the suggestion that they could name another issue. Even with the express invitation to pick an unnamed option, almost three-quarters chose one of the options offered. This result may not seem surprising until you learn that the four options offered were ones that had been mentioned as important by less than 1 per cent of respondents in an earlier survey. A good example of this type of problem in a real voting survey relates to the 1987 question on tactical voting. Respondents are given three options to explain the reason for their vote: 'I always vote that way; I thought it was the best party; I really preferred another party, but it had no chance of winning in this constituency' (Heath *et al.*, 1991, p.53). While the decisions not to use the term 'tactical voting' and to provide a range of responses to take attention away from that phenomenon are laudable, it is not clear that the resulting question is a good measure of tactical voting. There is also some evidence that not all respondents recognized the last option as a tactical vote: the writers report that some replied 'other', then said it was a tactical vote (Heath *et al.*, 1991, p.60). The three offered responses were not picking up all tactical voters. The fact that a majority chose one of the offered responses does not mean that another reply would not have been more popular if offered.

Central to the use of survey data is the assumption that everyone understands the question in the same way: all respondents and the researchers. When surveys are filled in by respondents they have no opportunity to ask for clarification and so may need to guess at what is meant. Even when the questions are asked by a trained interviewer, most companies instruct their staff not to interpret the questions for puzzled respondents as this may introduce a bias. Jackson (1992) has shown that clarifying key terms can change the results from a question because the ambiguous term was interpreted differently by different respondents.

A brief reading of the early surveys used will provide examples of ambiguity: 'Do you read a morning paper <u>regularly</u>?'; 'How much interest do you generally have in what's going on in <u>politics</u>?'; 'How close do you feel Britain's <u>ties</u> with America should be?...' [underlining added to indicate ambiguous word] (Butler and Stokes, 1974, pp.450; 451; 464). In the first example it is not clear if 'regularly' means daily, every Wednesday, twice a week or what. In the second example, 'politics' could mean the election, local government, international affairs or the latest gossip surrounding a prominent politician. In the third example it is not specified whether the 'ties' relate to politics, economics, trade, culture or what. Even the more recent surveys, while much improved, still contain some ambiguity (mainly in the newer questions), as in: 'Have the following gone too far or not far enough: the welfare benefits that are available to people today; spending by local councils'? [underlining added to indicate ambiguous word] (Heath *et al.*, 1991, p.279). People may vary in the type of payments they would consider as 'welfare benefits'. For example, some may have taken it to cover just income benefits, while others may include rent or rate rebates, mortgage relief, prescription charge reductions or pensioner bus passes. In the second example, again the type of spending considered may vary across the full range of a council's budget. Himmelweit's team provide another example when they ask if the question 'Do you like Thatcher?' means do you like her as a person, or as prime minister? (Himmelweit *et al.*, 1985, p.196). Other surveys are not exempt, but these examples serve to illustrate the point that ambiguous terms can easily creep into questionnaires.

Aside from some ambiguous terms, it is not clear that all questions, even habitually used ones, are interpreted in the same way by everyone. One common example will serve as a good illustration of possible problems: left–right, or thermometer scales. Respondents are frequently asked to place themselves and the political parties on a left–right scale, with varying levels of further information. In the early BES format, respondents were asked if they saw themselves on the left or the right, with no other explanation as to what these terms mean. In 1987 the British Communist Party and National Front were used as examples of the two ends of the scale. Although Butler and Stokes (1974, p.324) found that only a quarter of the respondents thought of themselves on a left–right scale, they nevertheless found the terms useful because they are flexible, can be open to different specific interpretations and can cover a range of things. This thinking, of course, is the total opposite of the idea that all must interpret a question in the same way for it to be useful. Heath's team also seem happy with the ability of respondents to understand the scales, based on the fact that they 'subjected a number of interviews to interaction coding analysis, which did not show up problems' (Heath *et al.*, 1985, p.103).

Problems with the use of scales are compounded by the evidence already presented about the willingness of respondents to accept the framework provided. As well as the common left–right scale, there has been increasing use of scales to ascertain views on key issues. Such questions give two positions that are placed at either end of a scale and respondents are then asked to place themselves and the parties along that scale. For example:

Some people feel that government should make much greater efforts to make people's incomes more equal. These people would put themselves in Box A. Other people feel that government should be much less concerned about how equal people's incomes are. These people would put themselves in Box K. And other people have views somewhere in between ... [under-lining in original]. (Heath *et al.*, 1991, p.274)

While this example provides alternatives that are intuitive opposites, not all such scales are so obviously 'balanced'. For instance, pitting 'protecting civil rights' against 'cutting crime' or 'cuts in tax' against 'increased spending on health and social security' (Heath *et al.*, 1991, pp.276; 271) is not necessarily providing the natural opposites.

Even when balanced and clearly understood labels are used for the ends of scales, the way in which the scale is marked may have an effect. A German team (Schwarz *et al.*, 1991) has done work on different responses when the numeric values on an otherwise identical scale are changed: using a '0 to 10' scale more people will place themselves at the lower end than if a '–5 to +5' scale is used. They conclude by suggesting that the use of negative values indicates a bipolar scale, while the other scale suggests shades of one opinion. Therefore the two scales should be used for the different types of attitude questions. People also differ in the range within the given scale they are likely to use, and have a tendency to stay in one part or the other, for example, always around the centre or always negative (Wilcox *et al.*, 1989). Scales present problems because of the need to have meaningful positions at each end; because of interpretation of those positions and the middle point and the difference between each point on the scale. While scales or 'thermometers' are widely used in voting behaviour studies, little is said about the possible problems related to the way in which respondents react to them.

The British Election Survey (BES)

Criticisms aimed at the BES in particular relate primarily to the emphasis on over-time comparability. Some objections concern the difficulty of achieving real comparability, while others question the emphasis placed upon the desire to do so. The repetition of questions across the years is seen as an important part of the BES, and the usefulness of such data is illustrated by the comparisons made by Heath's team in *Understanding Political Change* (Heath *et al.*, 1991). However, there is a limit to the number of questions that can be included in a survey, and the more room that is taken up with repetition of old questions, the less room is available for new questions and ideas: 'The replication of questions from one survey to the next may mean that bad traditions crowd out bold innovations; sloppily or inappropriately worded questions may be continued out of fear of breaking a time series while new measures – potentially the beginning of new time-series – are not adopted' (Crewe and Norris, 1992, p.9). While arguments about the need to take new directions are important for future studies, the reliability of repeated terms may be of more relevance to a critique of present studies.

For over-time comparison to work well, the questions must be measuring the same thing, but the above discussion of the effect of wording changes must ring warning bells. Even when wording is kept exact across surveys there are other problems both within and outside the control of the researchers. While some effort is made to keep wording the same, the context (place in the survey) must also be considered. There is evidence that the order in which questions are asked (Tourangeau *et al.*, 1989), the order in which responses are offered (Schuman and Presser, 1981) and the design of the survey (Sanchez, 1992) can change the responses. The importance of question ordering appears obvious for some issues, but there is evidence of more subtle influences too. For example, in a pair of questions on abortion, there was an expected increase in agreement when asking about abortion as a right before, rather than after, a question on abortion where there is 'a strong chance of serious defect in the baby' (Schuman and Presser, 1981, p.37). However, when replicating this experiment, evidence of the more subtle context effect of the placement of a general question on conservative or liberal views prior to the abortion questions was found

(Bishop *et al.*, 1986). This implies that changes to the order in which questions are asked can affect the responses given.

Even those authors who scrupulously report changes to question wording are unlikely to report changes in question order. A brief comparison of the 1979 and 1987 surveys, for instance, shows some changes of order. One example is that the question on how you voted is before the issue questions in the later survey, but after them in the earlier one: vote is question 41 in 1979 and question 8 in 1987. While the change may have been made for very sensible reasons, it is not mentioned in the texts, nor are any effects that may result from this change alluded to. This is one major example, but smaller ones where the effect may be just as great are also present. For instance, in a battery of questions in the 1979 BES, views on redistributing wealth come after those on how much should be spent on such areas as health and alleviating poverty, but in the 1987 BES the redistribution questions come before those on spending. Your views on taxation may differ depending on whether or not you have just said that more should be spent on health. In the same set of questions, views on the death penalty and stricter sentences are asked at the same time as views on state spending in 1979, and alongside views on respect and authority in 1987. Again, it seems likely that the context could alter the way in which the question was approached. Schuman and Presser are so concerned about context effects, that they warn that 'any attempt to compare marginal results from one survey to another ... should avoid re-moving a single question from a context of related terms, or else build in a way of assessing the effects of doing so' (1981, p.311). A precaution that does not appear to have been heeded in the BES studies.

Added to the problems of keeping questions the same, to aid comparability, is the counter problem of the changing nature of politics, which makes different issues topical and different aspects of issues contentious. A good example of an issue that has radically changed since the 1960s is nationalization (state ownership of companies). The standard question on nationalization that has been included in all surveys but one, asks if more or less companies should be nationalized. Not only does the status quo change in terms of which companies are nationalized, but now the vocabu-lary has also changed to one of privatization rather than national-ization. In light of all these changes, the long run of questions on nationalization must be interpreted in the light of the political situation at the time it was asked, and so cannot be considered as measuring exactly the same thing across the decades.

The emergence of new issues or forms of behaviour can also cause problems for comparability. For instance, Heath's team (Heath *et al.*, 1991, p.190) had to contend with a lack of environmental-type questions in early surveys, which meant having to make do with the few they could find that had some relevance. Similarly, there are no questions relating to tactical voting or even a second choice of party in the early surveys, so they took as tactical those who identify with one party but vote for another (Heath *et al.*, 1991, p.58). Factual, rather than attitudinal, questions can also suffer from external changes such as raising the school leaving age, changing the name of educational qualifications or the creation of the SDP and the Alliance. Heath's team in particular had to deal with many of these problems as they were analysing behaviour across the surveys.

When comparing results over time, a difference in results is usually taken as an indication of change in views, but might be due to variations in the way the data were collected. Schuman and Presser (1981, p.317) comment on the fact that in physical science there is a big emphasis on replication of results to show reliability, but this is not mirrored in survey research. Without the benefit of replication of measures taken at the same time, there is no clear evidence that an over-time change represents a change in the attitudes of the voters rather than a change in the usefulness of the measure. Simultaneous surveys are rare, due mainly to cost, so replication is difficult. Given these possible problems with reliable comparability over time, should the emphasis on repetition of questions be lessened? If not, then perhaps more effort should be made to ensure that only the year and the sample have changed.

Surveys are a useful tool, but their weaknesses must be taken into account. As one president of the American Association of Public Opinion Research suggested in his presidential address, limitations must be recognized and worked upon: 'therefore, we need both to remind ourselves and the public of the limitations of single variable results, and at the same time take whatever steps we can to reduce those limitations' (Schuman, 1986, p.442). A later president, Elinor Singer, went on to suggest real strategies for improving on the problems of question wording and context, but they take time, money and co-operation (Singer, 1988). While those studying voting behaviour continue to follow the orthodox approach to surveys with little criticism of each other and little serious consideration of the limitations of surveys as a tool, it seems unlikely that these suggested avenues of research will be followed in Britain.

Problems of Aggregate Data

Most data used in the study of voting behaviour, be it from surveys or other sources, are aggregated before analysis begins. This means that the responses from all the individuals are added together as a whole or in smaller meaningful groups, such as the voters in one constituency or all women or all of those who said that they voted for the Greens. Some form of aggregate data is used in most election studies. Reliance on aggregate measures shapes the type of questions that can be asked and the type of answers given. Worries relating to the use of aggregate data and to the limitations of the main sources of such data are covered here. Two concerns that arise from the use of aggregate data are the limitations of net measures and the perils of the ecological fallacy. In relation to reported census and voting statistics, the relevance of the units they use and problems of inadequate variables are discussed. Again, the whole debate cannot be fully covered, but key points and themes will be explored to illustrate the central point.

In analysis of survey data, the aggregated group is used to facilitate the comparison of the individuals who make up that group, so details about each member are retained. For example, the group of Conservative voters is compared to the group of Labour voters in terms of class or views on issues. Despite the advantage that surveys have of providing detailed information on individuals, the information is analysed as groups and subgroups. The aggregation of data to look at group behaviour is part of the orthodoxy:

Yet the whole of electoral analysis must not be focused on the individual citizen. The reasons for his behaviour often lie in a wider political or social milieu. Moreover, the consequences of individual change can be known only by aggregating the behaviour of individual electors to see what is true of the electorate as a whole. Electoral analyses demand both the reduction or disaggregation of mass phenomena to individual terms and also the aggregation of individual phenomena to explore effects in the full electorate. (Butler and Stokes, 1974, p.7)

With voting statistics or reported census data, only information about the new unit is provided, and details about individuals within the group are lost. For example, Appendix 1 in the book on the 1987 general election (Butler and Kavanagh, 1988, p.298) lists for the constituency of Liverpool Garston a Labour vote of 53.6 per cent, that 3.6 per cent have a university degree and that 45.7 per cent have a car, but we cannot tell if there is a Labour-voting graduate with a car. In this type of aggregate data the information is about the new, created unit, usually a constituency, and tells us what percentage of the people within that unit had a given characteristic.

Aggregating data provides net rather than overall or gross measures and this imposes constraints on the questions about voting behaviour that can be answered. Most writers acknowledge the problems with net measures, but one example illustrates the point: aggregate measures 'are inadequate for gauging the magnitude and direction of the various components of electoral change. The underlying pattern of vote switching is usually more complex than the net, visible movement suggested by the aggregate statistics' (Sarlvik and Crewe, 1983, p.32).

Given the percentage vote for each party at two successive elections, it is easy to calculate how many percentage points each party has gained or lost: these are the net changes. Again, the two measures, while relating to the same unit, do not cover the same people. The list of eligible voters in a constituency at any two elections will differ, for three main reasons. First, there are those who have moved in or out of the constituency, who may account for 20 per cent of registered voters each year (Rawlings, 1988, p.80), then there are those who were registered and have died and finally those who have reached voting age since the last election. Butler and Stokes (1974, p.242) calculated that this purely physical change in the total electorate meant that at least 16 per cent of 1959 electors had gone by 1970, and that at least 24 per cent of the 1970 voters had first registered since 1959. Therefore, net values would be affected if all existing voters voted the same way in both elections but all new voters voted differently from all voters who had gone. In this, somewhat unlikely, instance, the net change would be entirely due to the different views of the two groups and would exaggerate the extent to which individuals changed their vote.

An understatement of the extent to which individuals change how they vote is the more common complaint about net measures. Here the problem is that many individual switches are hidden because movement is not all one way, so countervailing switches can cancel each other out. For instance, five voters moving from Labour to the SNP will be cancelled out by five voters going from the SNP to Labour. Net values give the impression that one party gains votes and another loses them, but in a real election a party that loses overall will gain some new voters and a party that gains overall will lose some old voters. To gauge the extent of overall change, survey data must be used. Survey estimates for change between the two 1974 elections suggest that nearly a third of Liberals changed and about an eighth of Conservative and Labour voters (Himmelweit *et al.*, 1985, p.37), but the two-party net change for that election was 3 per cent with a net Liberal slip of 2 per cent (Sarlvik and Crewe, 1983, p.46). Of course, survey data are not without their problems (people are not always truthful about what they did), so the true extent of switching is still not precisely pinpointed. Nevertheless, the use of net measures of change mask the extent of overall change that occurs at the individual level. Reliance on net measures gives the impression of more stability than actually occurs and so helps to sustain the emphasis on explaining continuity rather than change.

Using the percentage of votes that were cast for each party along with certain social and economic characteristics for each constituency, analysts look for relationships between the two. Miller (1977, p.65) showed that there is a much stronger tie between class and vote at the constituency level than there is at the individual level. If you know the percentage of managers in a constituency, you have a good chance of predicting the percentage of votes won by the Conservatives. But, if, knowing this, you assume that managers are likely to vote Conservative, you commit the ecological fallacy: you assume knowledge about the individual from knowledge about the group. All analysts are aware of the problem, when using aggregate data to tell us about individual behaviour, of the ecological fallacy. While in this example it may seem intuitive to make such an inference, some cases are quite different. For instance, the 1987 increase in the percentage of votes for the Conservatives in areas with high 'New Commonwealth' levels should not suggest that members of that group vote Conservative, but that those living near them do: an anti-immigrant backlash (Johnston *et al.*, 1988, p.174). Aggregate measures tell us about the area as a whole, about the context for the voters; they should not be confused with individual characteristics. However, the context may well have an effect, like some whites living in areas with high immigrant populations having different attitudes towards immigration than similar whites living in areas with very low immigrant levels. Despite widespread recognition of the trap of an ecological fallacy, it is still very easy to fall into with careless use of language, as this example illustrates: '[the Alliance] no longer did particularly badly in the coalfields or among the unemployed and immigrants; it did lose white-collar votes in greater than expected numbers on the council estates...' (Johnston *et al.*, 1988, p.176). In this quote, descriptions of areas (coalfields, council estates) are mixed with individual characteristics (unemployed, immigrant, white-collar), although the aggregated census data which were used only give information on the areas. While this is a minor example, no doubt caused by problems of expression, it shows how an unwary reader could draw the wrong impression.

The two most common types of aggregate data used in voting behaviour studies are voting statistics and census reports, both of which are published for the constituency unit (although census data are also available for local government wards). Both of these datasets are constructed by government departments and so political scientists have no real influence over their collection or presentation. The way in which such data are produced is dictated by needs other than those of academic analysts and so they are not always in the optimum form for studying voting behaviour.

Census data are useful because they cover the entire population and are collected regularly, but the characteristics that are measured are not always the ones that those studying voting behaviour would find most useful. For instance, Johnston's team (Johnston *et al.*, 1988, p.165) mention that they cannot look at levels of coal mining separately because the census only gives an energy sector category. The most frequent complaint relates to measures of ethnic groups or immigrants, where researchers are forced to use measures like 'head of household born in the New Commonwealth or Pakistan' (Johnston *et al.*, 1988, p.168), which excludes third and subsequent generations of immigrants; children of 'mixed marriages' where the 'head of household' is British-born; and those from non-Commonwealth countries. Dunleavy and Husbands (1985, p.193) also comment on problems of measuring ethnic composition due to different measures being used in Scotland from those used in England and Wales. Other relevant variables, such as involvement in organizations like trade unions or parental characteristics, are not included in a census. The satisfactory comparison of the important measure of unemployment is also greatly hindered because of the numerous changes in the way it is measured. Between 1979 and 1988 there were nineteen changes in the way the official count of unemployed was defined (McIlroy, 1989, p.164). Therefore, some aspects of analysis are not possible because of the absence of a relevant census variable or because of problems with the way it is defined.

Mainly because of the lack of the desired measures, census variables are often used as surrogates. This substitution can lead to problems of interpretation. The discrepancy between the measure for 'blacks' outlined above, and what might usually be meant by the term, is a good example of how an imperfect measure has to stand for the characteristic under scrutiny. In these types of cases a characteristic is identified as being of interest, but there is no direct measure of it so another measure has to be substituted, which will tap only some of the desired attribute. Another, related problem with aggregate analysis is determining what the measures in use mean. For example, as Scarbrough (1987, p.238) points out, the usefulness of levels of agricultural workers in estimating Conservative vote levels cannot be the result of farm workers voting Conservative (there are not enough of them). Instead, the level of agricultural workers may correlate well with Conservative voting because it is an indicator of how rural the constituency is or how many large landowners there are, or some other relevant variable. Other measures are problematic because they are only measuring the same thing across the country in a superficial way. For example, the usefulness of 'percentage employed in manufacturing' as a predictor of vote differed in the north and south, but this may be because the type of manufacturing carried out in the two regions differs and so is really a different measure in each area (Scarbrough, 1987, p.238). In the end analysts are restricted to the variables that are included in the census and must make do the best they can.

Problems of measurement are not restricted to census data. Voting statistics relating to non-voters are not without problems, and may slightly exaggerate the level, whereas surveys underestimate it. Most of the problem in measuring non-voting from official statistics is the definition used. Non-voters are taken to be all those who are registered but did not vote. However, there are a number of other reasons why a person on the electoral roll did not vote: death; mistakenly on the list; moved away; voted elsewhere. British electoral rolls are a snapshot of residency on a day in October (usually the 10th) and come into use the following February

(Rawlings, 1988, Chapter 3), so the extent to which a roll is out of date will differ according to when the election is held. Also, while it is illegal to vote in more than one constituency, it is permissible to be registered in several places if residency can be proved in each place (Rawlings, 1988, Chapter 3). Therefore, all those registered in two places will count as a non-vote in one constituency even if they vote in the other. There is also some concern that the level of errors is getting worse so that, over time, the size of the error changes (Heath *et al.*, 1991, p.19). Comparing non-voting levels across areas at an election can also fall foul of the inaccuracy of this measure. Because there is more geographic movement of people in some areas than others, this will show as a regional difference in non-voting (Johnston *et al.*, 1988, p.22) and local authorities differ in the effort they make to find those who have not registered (Rawlings, 1988, p.91).

The relevance of using the constituency unit for understanding voting behaviour should also be questioned. While it is true that people's votes are used in a constituency to find the winner, that may be the only way in which that unit is meaningful to an individual. Behaviour within a constituency is the only thing that matters in terms of electing MPs, but behaviour may not be constrained by the same boundaries. The electoral boundaries are a construct for a given purpose and are created with certain criteria in mind, such as following local government boundaries (Rawlings, 1988, p.35). If these units, or the smaller local government wards, are used for aggregation, other, more important ones, such as meaningful neighbourhoods, cannot be examined (see Chapter 4). Here the problem is mostly due to the way in which these official statistics are published, and things have been improving. Indeed, the provision of census data in parliamentary constituency or local government ward units is relatively recent (Denver, 1989, p.123).

Presenting data for the constituency unit may give an unwarranted impression of similarity. One problem lies in the basis for measurement (or denominator) for calculating percentages of voting and census variables. Social measures for electorates, like employment rates, look at the percentage of the 'economically active' and so will exclude retired people (Dunleavy and Husbands, 1985, p.183) and include those between 16 and 18 who have left school (but are not eligible to vote). Therefore, the figure for 'professional and managerial' is taken as a percentage of a group that differs in several ways from the electorate. Not only are percentages based on different populations, but the actual people covered may also differ for the two sets of data. The census is conducted every 10 years and elections about every four years, so the most recent census may have been many years prior to the election and, due to population movement, may cover different people in that area. The last time that a full census was held in election year was 1951, and the election of 1992 was the closest to a census for some time. The major study using census data (Johnston *et al.*, 1988) looks at elections in 1979, 1983 and 1987, but uses census data for 1981: two years after the first election and six years before the last. Just because different variables are reported for each constituency does not mean that they are fully comparable.

Aggregated survey data are the normal source of information used in voting behaviour, but they are not problem-free. Some of the detailed problems with how questions are asked in surveys have been looked at, but little of this work is reported in studies of voting behaviour. Similarly, the problems associated with the use of aggregate data are not confronted in works that utilize such data. However, the orthodox methodology can have an effect on the way in which voting behaviour is understood, as the next section illustrates.

Two Case Studies

Space does not permit a full cataloguing of the detailed consequences of the orthodox methodology, but two different areas will serve as examples. The orthodox methodology is challenged by showing some of its limitations. First, groups and ideas that are routinely ignored or set aside because of the source of data or method of analysis are examined. One problem in looking to see which groups are systematically excluded is that you do not always notice that they are not there, and sometimes you only notice when someone mentions them. Of course, it is impossible to reference the exclusion of something unless the author specifically mentions it. Therefore those who admit to excluding a group and those who start to include a previously excluded group will, of necessity, be the focus of attention. Second, the popular measure of 'swing' is examined to show how an orthodox statistical tool can shape analysis. Swing has come in for criticism since it was first used, but is still to be found in many accounts of elections. These two case studies show different ways in which the orthodox methodology affects the study of voting behaviour.

Who is excluded?

Various types of individuals are excluded from election studies because of the orthodox assumptions, approaches, idea of what is of interest and method of classification. Different groups are excluded in a variety of ways. For example, non-voters are often omitted (although Butler and Stokes included them), as are minor party voters, because of the concentration on Conservative and Labour voters (see discussion in Chapter 2). Class classification norms have hindered full analysis of women and the unemployed or those dependent on state benefits. Definition of the sample to be taken for the surveys leads to the exclusion of Northern Ireland and the north of Scotland (only electorates in Wales, England and Scotland south of the Caledonian Canal are used). Methods of analysis and the desire to achieve a 'good fit' lead to the occasional exclusion of other groups, again often Liberal and other small party voters. Reliance on national surveys for the main data means that small groups cannot be studied, such as distinct ethnic groups or Scottish and Welsh Nationalists. The desire to find general trends focuses attention on what are deemed to be normal voters, and away from all other groups.

Excluding non-voters from analysis applies mainly to studies based on survey data (Rose and McAllister, 1986; Dunleavy and Husbands, 1985; Himmelweit et al., 1985; Heath et al., 1985; Heath et al., 1991). Those who use aggregate data (Johnston et al., 1988) or include an analysis of the flow of the vote (Butler and Stokes, 1974, Chapter 12; Sarlvik and Crewe, 1983, Chapter 2) recognize the importance of non-voting as a category of behaviour. The few detailed studies that have been done on non-voting are separate from the core texts (see Denver and Hands, 1992, p.17). Ignoring non-voters is excused by some (Heath et al., 1991, p.19) because of studies (Crewe et al., 1977; Swaddle and Heath, 1989) that show that most non-voters were 'accidental' abstainers due to illness or being on holiday. However, both of these studies checked reports of voting against the register of votes issued for one election only. American studies, while showing higher levels of non-voting and false reporting of the vote in a survey, checked reported voting over several elections and found not only consistent non-voters, but also consistent mis-reporters (Presser and Traugott, 1992). Even if the abstention was not intended, it is part of the behaviour of voters on election day and should be covered in analysis.

Even those who include non-voters for some analyses may exclude them for others, such as tree analysis or multiple regression (for example Sarlvik and Crewe, 1983, pp.104; 164). The identification of sufficient non-voters in survey data for satisfactory analysis is a problem exacerbated by the tendency of some non-voters to say they have voted, and for non-voters to be more prevalent among those who refuse to participate in a survey than among those who agree (Swaddle and Heath, 1989, pp.539–40). With turnout rates in the low seventies, up to a quarter of the registered electorate may be abstaining, and there are also those who do not register although eligible to do so. These people, by not voting, are expressing a view about politics: be it apathy, disaffection or complacency. If large numbers of normal abstainers decide to vote or large numbers of normal voters decide to abstain, the end result of the election can be altered. Therefore, understanding the motivation to choose an abstention rather than a party must be part of the overall interpretation of voting behaviour.

The main way in which women have been ignored relates to their class classification. Married women were routinely categorized according to their husband's occupation (Butler and Stokes, 1969, p.70; Rose and McAllister, 1986, p.39; Sarlvik and Crewe, 1983, p.75). Later writers (Heath *et al.*, 1985, p.22; Dunleavy and Husbands, 1985, p.125) have abandoned this practice and place all people in the class that relates to their own occupation. However, the division is not just one of chronology, for Rose and McAllister (1986) defend the habit of giving a household rather than a person [married woman] a class, and describe the class per person method as an 'innovation' (p.46). They go on to argue that only 10 per cent of the electorate have a different class from their spouse, so classification by head of household is not a big problem (p.72). A person who is not working and has not worked is still given a 'household' class, but only since 1979 have economically inactive men been asked what their wives do (Heath *et al.*, 1991, p.82 n5).

Hiding women as individuals also has implications for the meaning of other variables. In particular, class and trade union membership are both affected by gender, with women disproportionately in the non-manual rather than manual class and in public sector, non-manual trade unions (Dunleavy and Husbands, 1985, pp.125; 131). Again this norm can be linked to the ease of the orthodoxy. Dunleavy and Husbands point out that 'Using a husband's class measure to categorise a married woman has a number of useful implications for conventional explanations. For one thing, it produces a very evenly matched spread of men and women across occupational classes' (Dunleavy and Husbands, 1985, p.125). Another consequence of using the class of the man is that parental class influence is taken from the father (for example, Rose and McAllister, 1986, p.103). All of these practices are based on assumptions about women, their social location and political influences that are both untested and unstated. Although women are over half of the electorate, studies are based on the 'male as norm' model.

Another group generally left out by the traditional class categorization are those who are not working. While there is much disagreement about the proper way to distinguish between classes (see Chapter 4), none provides a clear category for those who are not working. In general, people who are unemployed are classed according to the last job they had, or failing that, by the class of their spouse; if both are missing they are left undefined and so are excluded from the schema. Even accurately identifying those who are unemployed or receiving welfare benefits may be difficult in a survey because of the perceived stigma attached to those situations (Dunleavy and Husbands, 1985, p.144). Increased unemployment levels may also affect other variables related to work status, such as trade union membership (Dunleavy and Husbands, 1985, p.131; Rose and McAllister, 1986, p.57) or income (Heath *et al.*, 1991, p.157; Rose and McAllister, 1986, p.62). Again there is the problem of looking at an unemployed individual or a family with an unemployed person as the 'head of household'.

Sometimes a group of voters is excluded from one piece of analysis in an attempt to 'improve the fit'. Most multivariate analyses seek to show a relationship between several independent variables and one dependent variable: for example, using a range of issue attitudes to explain a Conservative vote. Such techniques produce a measure of fit which indicates how well the independent variable(s) explain the dependent variable. The bigger the measure of fit, the better the explanation or model; so a big value is prized. Sometimes judicious manipulation of the variables used will produce a better fit. Such a move is very tempting, but means the analysis then excludes groups that do not fit the overall pattern. The following two examples illustrate the point: '1964 and 1970 were the exceptional ones [elections]. And if those two elections are excluded from the analyses, the assumption of constant odds ratios turns out to give a perfectly acceptable fit' (Heath *et al.*, 1985, p.35); 'When we omitted the Liberals from the analyses, we could "predict" Conservative and Labour votes with close to 90% accuracy' (Himmelweit *et al.*, 1985, p.86). Rather than studying the 'odd' results to aid understanding, they are removed to facilitate the measurement of general trends.

Other studies exclude particular cases from the analysis because of problems of suitable data. For instance, when looking at the effect of women candidates on the vote, Dunleavy and Husbands (1985, p.204) had to exclude 15 constituencies where there were two women standing from the major parties because their comparison method to test for a gender effect could not be used there. In their study of 'Great Britain', Johnston's team (Johnston *et al.*, 1988, p.251) omit the regions of 'Devon and Cornwall' and 'North Rural' from analysis because the cells for these areas were too small to use reliably in cross-tabulation tables. In all cases the authors admit the omission, but tend to proceed with the analysis as if there were not any such gaps. There is no knowing if the inclusion of the omitted cases would have changed the overall results.

Having too small a number of people from key groups in a dataset is a common problem with surveys because the data are collected to represent the whole country. When a group is small in size or geographically concentrated within Britain, a sample designed to represent Britain as a whole will contain few people from that group. But just because a group is small in size does not mean that it is not interesting or important in terms of understanding voting behaviour. In this category of excluded cases, the most commonly mentioned groups are blacks (for example, Dunleavy and Husbands, 1985, p.121; Heath *et al.*, 1991, p.112) and voters for small parties (for example, Sarlvik and Crewe, 1983, p.38; Rose and McAllister, 1986, p.164). Most works exclude small parties such as the Nationalists without even mentioning the fact (for example, Dunleavy and Husbands, 1985; Heath *et al.*, 1985; Himmelweit *et al.*, 1985). Again the desire for nationwide trends means that distinct groups cannot be adequately studied.

Other characteristics have been widely ignored because early studies suggested they were not important: 'Because in the early studies those not identified with any party were found to be badly informed, little involved in politics and disinterested in the outcome of elections, for many years political scientists devoted hardly any attention to them' (Himmelweit *et al.*, 1985, p.192).

Similarly, religion has only recently been considered (Heath *et al.*, 1991, pp.85–8) and regional differences are either ignored or taken as a sign of how 'un-British' those bits of the country are (Rose and McAllister, 1986, p.33). None of the studies considers other types of election behaviour, such as for local government or by-elections. Tracing this last practice back to the Michigan studies, Butler and Stokes (1974) said it was difficult to look at regions with national survey data (p.126); they ignored those who did not give a con- sistent view on the range of issues (p. 316); and they considered religion to be an old and declining alignment (Chapter 7).

Decisions about what to examine and how it is to be defined fre- quently relate back to previous studies, so that a norm is established. However, such a practice can systematically exclude certain groups from the analysis. In this way, the general approach to deciding which variables are useful constrains the study of voting behaviour. Clearly the methodological concentration on general trends and a nationwide survey means that only those things that are seen as 'mainstream' are included in the study. Having to rely on census data adds to the problem of including some groups in analysis.

Is swing meaningful?

Of the many measures traditionally used in the study of elections, swing is probably the most widely known. Comments about the extent of swing at an election or the size of swing needed for a certain party to win are commonplace. Denver and Hands describe it as the 'single statistic which succinctly summarises electoral change' (1992, p.3), which is of course the primary focus of ortho- dox studies of voting behaviour. However, the widespread use of swing does not mean that it is free from problems and arguments. Rather, swing is far from the straightforward measure many assume it to be.

An examination of swing provides a useful example of how a particular method or tool, even a 'crude' one, can take hold and shape both the method of analysis and the understanding of voting behaviour. From journalistic reports and a casual reading of the texts, it would appear that swing is a widely understood term. However, a careful perusal of the footnotes in election studies texts soon unveils a more complex situation involving several different ways of calculating swing (see Table 3.1). The main ones are set out in an appendix (pages 76 to 78), with the value of the change between the 1987 and 1992 elections for each one. While its calculation has been described as simple (Denver, 1989, p.18), an ability to deal with negative numbers is vital. Detailed calculations for the 1987 to 1992 swing, using the different formulae, are also given in the appendix to this chapter.

Table 3.1 Definitions of 'swing'

Butler or 'traditional swing': the change in the Conservative share of the vote plus the change in the Labour share of the vote, divided by two. But if both parties gain or lose, the Labour value is subtracted from the Conservative one, then halved. (Negative values = swing to Labour)

Steed or 'two-party swing': the change in the Conservative share of the two-party (Labour and Conservative) vote.

Overall swing: calculated for the country as a whole, so takes the percentage of the overall vote won by Conservative and Labour.

Mean swing: calculated for each constituency separately, with the results then averaged for the whole country. Sometimes median swing is used also (the middle value).

Pederson Index or 'index of dissimilarity': adds the percentage change for each party (ignoring signs), then divides by two. Gives the proportion of voters who would need to change to make results for both elections the same.

As with other aspects of the orthodoxy examined earlier, a major problem with swing is what it misses out. In particular, those who do not vote for the leading parties are ignored. While each of the different measures can be calculated to include the effect of non-voting (see Table 3.2), this is not normally done. The concentration on the decision of which party is voted for again excludes consideration of the decision not to vote and the effect this can have on the overall result. Votes for third or minor parties are also traditionally excluded, although this is not universal. The Nuffield study of each election has, since 1955, only given the constituency swing where Conservative and Labour are the top two candidates (Butler and Kavanagh, 1988, p.285), which covered 296 (47 per cent) of the 634 constituencies in Britain in 1992. Even prior to the rise of the Alliance (now Liberal Democrats), Conservative–Labour contests were not always the norm: in Scotland in 1979, swing is only given for 16 of the 71 seats and 10 of them were against the 'national' flow (Butler and Kavanagh, 1979, Appendix 1). The reason given for only including Conservative–Labour contests and sticking with the older measure of (Butler) swing in the tables of Appendix 1 is to allow for comparison over time. Other publications (Linton, 1992) calculate constituency swing for the top two parties in each constituency. And, while they ignore movements among other options, they do at least recognize the number of contests where a party other than Conservative or Labour came first or second.

While early on Butler (1951, p.315) recognized the problem for swing of contests that included a Liberal, he suggested that they drew votes equally from the two major parties and so had no effect on their relative strength. More recently it has been shown that third party votes do not move equally to the major parties, partly due to tactical voting which would result in a disproportionate move to the second-placed party (Curtice and Steed, 1982, p.265). Or, as Rose and McAllister (1986, p.3) point out: 'Those who have learnt the intricacies of calculating the swing of votes between the Labour and Conservative parties may do this in more and more refined ways, even though the great movement of votes in 1983 was not a swing between the major parties but a shift from both the Labour and Conservative parties to the Alliance.' Even when Britain clearly did not resemble a two-party system, the idea of swing between the two 'major' parties held sway.

The idea of swing also gives the impression of movement in one direction only. On the constituency level, because it is another net measure, swing hides all counter movements that individual voters make. On the countrywide level, an overall measure of swing gives the impression that the movement is in the same direction in all constituencies. Even in an election when movement is predominantly one way, such as in 1979, some seats will move the other way: 17 of the swings shown were to Labour (Butler and Kavanagh, 1979, Appendix 1). Also, as the description of Butler swing (above) indicates, sometimes both major parties may see a gain or loss in votes, but swing will still be calculated: 'This "swing" [of 2 per cent to Labour] is only a technical one: the Conservative vote share actually increased (+3 per cent) but Labour's increased by even more (+7 per cent)' (Sarlvik and Crewe, 1983, p.86). In this case, talking of a 'swing to' anyone does not reflect reality.

Part of the reason why swing caught on as a concept was that early elections showed a 'uniform swing' across the country. So, in 1955 the swing is described as 'still very uniform' (Butler, 1955, p.160), and almost two decades later Butler and Stokes comment on the 'remarkable uniformity of swings in party support across all constituencies...' (1974, p.7). But how uniform is it really when a range of 5 per cent covers only three-quarters of constituencies, as was the case in 1955 (Butler, 1955, p.202)? And, as Rasmussen (1965, p.448) asks, can swing be seen as uniform when the range needed to cover 90 per cent of constituencies includes those whose swing is in the opposite direction? To use a uniform swing figure validly to represent the whole country, there must be an assumption of little regional variation (Rasmussen, 1965, p.446), but this is increasingly not the case (for example, Sarlvik and Crewe, 1983, p.31; Heath *et al.*, 1985, Chapter 6; Johnston *et al.*, 1988, Chapter 1).

There is also a major conceptual challenge to the interpretation of uniform swing that depends on the difference between actual and proportionate change (Berrington, 1965). A uniform swing from the Conservative party of 4 per cent would mean that in each constituency the Conservative vote would go down by around four percentage points. In a seat where the Conservatives held 20 per cent of the vote, this would drop to 16 per cent, and where they held 40 per cent, this would decrease to 36 per cent. But, in the first case this decrease was a fifth of the original vote, while in the second it was a tenth: a different proportion of the original Conservative vote left that party, but it gave a uniform swing. Therefore, the impression of uniform swing is deceptive, because the size of the group that moved in each area differs.

Despite recognized flaws with the measure, swing is still used regularly by journalists, politicians and academics when talking about elections. A frequent academic defence of this use is that swing is a useful tool for comparison across time (Butler and Stokes, 1974, p.248) or areas (McLean, 1980, p.63). Regional variations are turned into a virtue, and comparison of constituency and mean swing is used to show which constituencies are vastly different (Butler and King, 1966, p.351; Butler and Kavanagh, 1992, pp.324–32). Heavy reliance on swing as a way of talking about changes from one election to another has encouraged the orthodox methodological tendency towards the net or overall picture and a concentration on votes cast for the major parties. This is but one example of how a normal statistical method has helped to exclude groups from the picture when elections and voting behaviour are analysed.

Summary

The orthodox methodology covers both the way in which data are collected and how they are used. Common to the main voting behaviour studies is the use of aggregate data gathered using survey techniques. The emphasis on general trends across the country plays a major part. Within the central BES series there is an added emphasis on continuity that has helped to shape the direction of enquiries. Looking at the two case studies of those groups which are excluded from analysis, and the use of the measure of swing, illustrates the limitations imposed by the orthodox methodology. Considering the most notable groups that are normally excluded from analysis shows how debate is channelled down certain paths, and examining the arguments relating to the idea of swing highlights the way in which the use of specific statistical techniques can impose limitations on what is considered. Both case studies highlight particular problems, but similar results could be emphasized if other aspects of the voting behaviour methodology were examined. The case studies serve to illustrate the type of limitations that can occur due to the orthodox methodology. Broad criticisms of the conduct of surveys and the way in which they are utilized suggest some of the problems with the orthodox methodology. Limitations of aggregate data point up other consequences. In both cases there are a series of detailed criticisms, but the central point is that the studies within the orthodoxy do not address these questions nor even mention their existence.

In this examination of aspects of the orthodox methodology the emphasis on over-time comparability stands out. While the desire to understand each election in comparison to previous contests is both sound and understandable, creeping conservatism may also play a part in the great emphasis placed on comparability. An early explanation as to why the definition of swing could not change serves to illustrate this point. Butler (1965, p.52) explained that in psephology 'statistical work is quickly popularised', so 'the definition of swing based on the total vote has got into the minds of politicians and the press' to such an extent that he is 'sceptical about the wisdom of trying to re-educate an easily confused group of people to a new definition'. While the old is kept to avoid the pain of introducing the new, the orthodox methodology will continue.

Readers may be surprised to have reached the end of this chapter without hitting vast arrays of equations or statistical signs. What has been covered here mostly relates to concepts rather than detailed statistics. However, much of the detailed argument that goes on among psephologists, the battle within the orthodox framework, relates to statistical arguments. They argue about how to operationalize the orthodox position, rather than questioning it. Consequently the concepts and constructs are not questioned while the illusion of fierce debate continues. Authors argue about different ways to use aggregate measures derived from survey questions without pondering the limitations of those measures. More and more complex techniques are utilized, but fundamental questions about the effects of the orthodox methodology go unasked.

Appendix – Calculations of Swing

Table 3.2 Vote share for 1987 and 1992 British general elections

	1987 (As % of)		1992 (As % of)	
	Votes cast	Registered voters	Votes cast	Registered voters
Conservative	42.2	31.8	41.9	32.6
Labour	30.8	23.2	34.4	26.7
Liberal Democrat	22.6	17.0	17.8	13.9
Nationalists	1.7	1.3	2.4	1.7
Others	2.7	2.0	3.5	2.8
Non-vote	NA	24.7	NA	22.3

Table 3.3 Different measures of 'swing', 1987–1992

	Normal measure	Including non-voters
Butler swing		
Con and Lab	−1.95	−1.35
Con and LD	2.25	1.95
Lab and LD	4.2	3.3
Two-party swing	−2.9	NA
Mean Butler swing	−2.5	
Pederson Index	5.1	4.3

Butler swing between party A and party B

(Party A 2nd contest – Party A 1st contest) plus (Party B 1st contest – Party B 2nd contest) all divided by 2

Conservative and Labour

Conservative   (% 1992 – % 1987)   = (41.9 – 42.2)   =   -0.3
Labour   (% 1987 – % 1992)   = (30.8 – 34.4)   =   -3.6

therefore swing is (-0.3 + (-3.6) ÷ 2   =   -1.95
Value is negative therefore swing is to party B, in this case Labour.

Conservative and Liberal Democrats

Conservative   (% 1992 – % 1987)   = (41.9 – 42.2)   =   -0.3
Liberal Democrat (% 1987 – % 1992)   = (22.6 – 17.8)   =   4.8

therefore swing is (-0.3 + 4.8) ÷ 2   =   2.25
Value is positive therefore swing is to party A, in this case the Conservatives.

Labour and Liberal Democrats

Labour   (% 1992 – % 1987)   = (34.4 – 30.8)   =   3.6
Liberal Democrat (% 1987 – % 1992)   = (22.6 – 17.8)   =   4.8

therefore swing is (3.6 + 4.8) ÷ 2   =   4.2
Value is positive therefore swing is to party A, in this case Labour.

Two-party swing

The change in the Conservative share of the two-party vote.
First find the number of votes cast for the Conservatives and Labour in each election:
Conservative 1987 + Labour 1987 = 13,763,066 + 10,029,778
= 23,792,844
Conservative 1992 + Labour 1992 = 14,092,891 + 11,559,735
= 25,652,626

Conservative share of two-party vote is:
1987: (13,763,066 ÷ 23,792,844) × 100 = 57.8
1992: (14,092,891 ÷ 25,652,626) × 100 = 54.9

Change in Conservative share is:
1992–1987 = 54.9 – 57.8 = -2.9

Pederson Index

Add the change in percentage for each party, ignoring signs, then
halve.

For each party, % in 1992 minus % in 1987:

Conservative $41.9 - 42.2 \ = -0.3$
Labour $34.4 - 30.8 \ = \ \ 3.6$
Liberal Democrat $17.8 - 22.6 \ = -4.8$
Nationalists $2.4 - 1.7 \ \ \ = \ \ 0.7$
Others $3.5 - 2.7 \ \ \ = \ \ 0.8$

then add all values, regardless of positive or negative sign, and halve
the total:

$(0.3 + 3.6 + 4.8 + 0.7 + 0.8) \div 2 = 5.1$

4

Framing Fierce Debate

The previous chapters have considered aspects of the orthodox approach and methodology using the entire mainstream field of voting behaviour. However, the component models within the field do differ. This chapter considers how these models and arguments between the different authors are framed within the confines of the orthodoxy. There are a number of particularly contentious issues that account for much of the disagreement between models, and this chapter looks at three of them. Two relate to widely recognized concepts that were discussed in Political Change in Britain (Butler and Stokes, 1974): party identification and class voting. Each concept, although widely recognized, generates deep argument over details, relevance and measurement. The third debate centres on the idea of a context or neighbourhood effect. This idea, which relates back to the local neighbourhood work in the Columbia model discussed in Chapter 1, is less widely recognized, but still hotly contested.

These three concepts are mentioned in most of the works on voting behaviour studied here. Although 'fierce debate' centres around these ideas, the discussion is still confined by the orthodox framework. In the following sections each concept is covered separately by first outlining the basis of each argument, then looking at ways in which it is affected by the orthodoxy. Not only do the orthodox approach and methodology limit the way in which these concepts are explored, they also cause some of the arguments and major points of contention.

Party Identification

Partisan self-image, or party identification as it is now more commonly known, is central to the early models of voting behaviour, but later works also pay much attention to the idea. Some (Dunleavy and Husbands, 1985; Rose and McAllister, 1986) try to show that the concept no longer, if ever, has great relevance, while others (Heath *et al.*, 1991, p.200) are less harsh. However, probably predictably, definitions of the key term vary. Although the label is maintained, the exact concept and interpretation differs. Central to the concept of party identification, as used in the original American studies, was the idea of an enduring, inherited, emotive attachment to a political party that would withstand occasional voting deviations (Berelson *et al.*, 1954, p.121 and p.147). In the journey across the Atlantic some of these aspects were changed and others have been altered over the years.

Butler and Stokes stress the enduring nature of the attachment: '... most electors think of themselves as supporters of a given party in a lasting sense, developing what might be called a "partisan self-image"' (1974, p.39). Both the psychological and the inherited aspects of partisan self-image are discussed more in relation to class than political attitudes (p.95). The independence of partisan attachment and vote in America was discussed at some length (pp.39–43), but in the end the authors concluded that '... partisan self-image and electoral preferences travel together in Britain far more than in America' (p.42).

For Sarlvik and Crewe (1983), 'being ready to adopt a party label may be taken as an expression of a more generalised attitude' (p.293), which 'often forms a lasting element in a person's political outlook' (p.295). However, there is some movement on the idea of acceptable deviation between vote and attachment: 'most electors naturally vote in accordance with their general sense of partisanship. But electoral choice and party identification do not have entirely the same meaning' (p.296). In describing the original party identification model Himmelweit's team mentioned the elements of 'stability', adolescent socialization, 'predisposition' and acceptable 'lapses' (Himmelweit *et al.*, 1985, p.4). However, they reject the pre-eminence of party identification in explaining vote choice and instead see it as:

more appropriate to follow the dictum, 'action speaks louder than words', and to concentrate in voting studies on the forces within society and within the parties that influence vote choice. Such analysis would include party identification as a summary statement of the voters' general political preferences which, as suggested in the cognitive model of vote choice, would interact with their preferences on specific issues and candidates. (Himmelweit *et al.*, 1985, p.194)

Johnston's team describe the traditional model as one where:

choice is a product of Social Attributes, as mediated by Political Ideology and Party Identification. As people grow into adulthood having particular social attributes so they develop political ideologies linked to those attributes, as part of the socialisation process. Those ideologies, in turn, lead them to identify with particular political parties; again, this is usually part of the socialisation process, so that assuming the ideology of a particular social group involves, among other things, accepting that one particular party is linked to that ideology and is the one they should support. And finally, having identified with a particular party then they habitually vote for it. (Johnston *et al.*, 1988, p.220)

Thus the enduring, emotive and inherited aspects are mentioned, but not the acceptability of occasional deviations in behaviour.

Dunleavy and Husbands also include enduring, emotive and inherited factors in their description of the original model: 'Most voters develop long-run, emotive or habitual "identifications" with one party...' and 'people tend to form their political views quite early... under the dominant influences of their parents and their family's social environment' (1985, p.4). However, they also omit the acceptance of occasional deviations from the original construct. Indeed, they see such a difference as a problem and 'are sceptical of the meaning that should be attached to this concept, especially when voting decisions and "party identification" are often inconsistent, as in our survey' (p.95). Rose and McAllister follow the same pattern, mentioning the 'persistence of parental influence' and the resulting 'consistent judgements' in their description of the original model (1986, p.104). Their criticism also relates to the closeness between voting and identification, but takes the contrary line that because the correlation is so close, party identification is a tautology (p.132).

Heath and his colleagues also describe the original model in terms of 'stable attachments' that 'performed the psychological function of helping the voter cope with political information and the complexities of politics' (Heath *et al.*, 1991, p.11). They also recognize the importance of childhood socialization (p.38). In their first book, this team recognized that 'people remain attached to their previous parties even when they have moved out of line with them on major political principles' (Heath *et al.*, 1985, p.123). However, the idea of a deviation between the vote and party identification is not accepted. They measure tactical voting by taking all those who identify with one party and vote for another (Heath *et al.*, 1991, p.58), suggesting that this can be the only reason for such incongruence.

Common to perceptions of 'party identification' is the idea of a learnt, long-term attachment, but the original and central acceptance of a voting deviation is absent. Many of the later criticisms of party identification concern the perceived closeness of the tie between vote and allegiance. Rather than acting as a background influence to the vote, identification may itself be affected by voting, so that the two 'travel together' (Aimer, 1989) and therefore both measure partisanship. So, does a difference between vote and identification tell us that party identification is useful or that it is badly measured, or that the 'acceptable deviation' component of the original American model must be resurrected? The other main area of criticism questions the preeminence of party identification and instead suggests that it is one of a series of relevant influences (for example, Himmelweit *et al.*, 1985).

Having set out the main descriptions of party identification and outlined the key arguments, the question of the effect of the orthodox approach arises. Can the problems or arguments be 'blamed' on the orthodoxy? Some of the arguments relate to the measurement of party identification, but others are concerned with interpretation. Therefore both the approach and methodology aspects of the orthodox position, covered in Chapters 2 and 3, may have an effect.

There are two main strands to arguments about the measurement of party identification in surveys. In a general assault on the use of the traditional survey question, doubts are raised about the ability to tap the enduring quality of party identification as distinct from the vote. More specifically, the way in which the original American question has been used elsewhere with the omission of an 'independent' category is queried. The original party identification question used by the Michigan team asks, 'Generally speaking do you usually think of yourself as a Republican, a Democrat, an Independent, or what?' (Johnston, 1992, p.546). However, when transporting this question it had to be changed to suit the local situation. The 'independent' part was removed as that concept has no meaning in Britain. Rather than replace 'independent' with another opt-out clause, Butler and Stokes felt that most respondents would take a partisan label (1974, p.44). So, British respondents were asked, 'Generally speaking do you usually think of yourself as Conservative, Labour, Liberal or what?' (Butler and Stokes, 1974, p.470). This practice was followed by successive custodians of the British Election Survey (BES), although other studies have utilized different approaches, for instance, Dunleavy and Husbands started with the filter question, 'Generally speaking, do you think of yourself as closer to one of the parties than to the others?' (1985, p.95), and then asked those who said 'yes' which party that was.

Johnston (1992) looks at the effect of not having a 'nonpartisan' option in party identification questions used outside the USA. He found that the percentage not identifying with a party was highest when 'or none of these' was added at the end of the question (p.551). Not specifying a non-identification option bolsters the number of identifiers. Interestingly, in relation to the discussion in the previous chapter, Johnston also found some evidence of a context effect, with higher levels of identification when respondents were asked about the vote before the identification question (p.554). This finding has relevance because the voting question precedes the party identification question in the BES surveys. If a prior question about the recent act of voting can affect identification levels, then the ability of the classic question to tap enduring attachment must be examined (for recent debate see McAllister and Wattenberg, 1995; Heath and Pierce, 1992).

Two aspects of the orthodox methodology seem to be influencing the measurement of party identification. First, the general disregard for detailed examination of the importance of providing an opt-out clause and the possibility of context effects may have produced a question that maximizes levels of identification. Added to this, the general desire to maintain consistency dampens any question of changing the standard format. The common practice of including as identifiers those who denied an identity but, in the follow-up question, said that they were 'closer to' a party, surely dilutes the potency of the core variable too. So a reported range of attachments to a party is condensed into identifiers and non-identifiers. Again a tendency to create dichotomous variables may be obscuring some of the meaning of the variable under consideration. Butler and Stokes established the boundaries for the measurement of party identification in Britain that have been followed since.

The more general concern is that the classic party identification question does not measure the concept. One worry is that the enduring aspect may not be perceived by respondents and so the measure becomes synonymous with the vote. Although the phrases 'generally speaking' and 'usually' are included to broaden the time frame (Converse, 1976, p.35), it is not clear that respondents pick up on these cues, especially when they have just been asked a long series of questions about the recent election. There have been studies arguing that people change their vote more than their identification (Denver,

1989, p.29), but others argue that party identification predicts vote
so well it may really be just another way of measuring the same thing
(Johnston, 1992, p.544). On the one hand are arguments that there
is such a discrepancy between the two that party identification
cannot be a useful explanation of voting (for example, Dunleavy
and Husbands, 1985). On the other hand are those, like Rose and
McAllister (1986), who see voting and party identification as two
sides of the same coin because of the close correlation between the
two. That the two sets of authors have diametrically opposed views on
the closeness of fit between vote and identification may well be a
result of the different questions that were used to measure party
identification. The arguments continue, but it would seem that the
solution lies in qualitative research surrounding the survey question
and how respondents interpret it, rather than ever more complex
statistical analysis of the variables.

In Chapter 2 the orthodox approach was described as covering the
aims, interpretation and main areas of study. The understanding and
use of party identification are closely tied with the 'vote as support'
assumption discussed as part of the orthodox interpretation. In using
identification there is also a tendency to concentrate on the major
parties and on identifiers, so following the orthodox line on what to
study. Although some early mention is made of the problems facing
Liberal identifiers when the party does not field a full slate of candidates, and when they are likely to lose, this area is not consistently
studied. Similarly, those who do not identify tend to be marginalized.
The survey questions first try to push such people into some sort of
identification with the follow-up question on which party they feel
closer to. In analysis, the small group who maintained a detachment
from the parties are not investigated in any depth. Again the main
group is put under the microscope and the 'deviants' ignored. Thus
any chance of learning by comparison is lost.

By losing the acceptance of a voting deviation from an otherwise
enduring identification, the expected tie between identification and
vote becomes stronger. But if there is an expectation that the vote will
not deviate from identification, why is it necessary to distinguish
between the two? Party identification as a lasting predisposition
which survives short-term lapses should show differences from the
vote, but is difficult to measure at election time. Party identification as
an habitual and constant adherence to a party should not differ from
vote and is easier to measure at election time. It seems that the latter
is what is commonly used. The prominence of the idea of 'support'

comes through in the general interpretations of party identification. Although the basic question never uses the word 'support', those who say they are identifiers are often described as supporters (for example, Sarlvik and Crewe, 1983, p.293; Denver, 1989, p.29; Rose and McAllister, 1986, p.155). So party identification seems to be active patronage of a party rather than a more general partisan disposition. Thus, the vote is seen as synonymous with identification; the former is the action the other the feeling. If party identification is seen as support and the vote mirrors party identification, then the orthodox reading of a vote as support makes sense. But if vote and party identi-fication are not synonymous and/or to identify with a party does not mean you want to promote all it stands for, then a vote is not a sign of support. In part the orthodox view of 'vote as support' can be blamed on common conceptions of party identification.

Class Voting

Class is probably the variable that is most frequently utilized by academics and others involved in the explanation of voting behavi-our. This emphasis started early: 'Class has long been pre-eminent among the factors used to explain party allegiance in Britain' (Butler and Stokes, 1974, p.67). However, the frequent use of class as an explanation for voting does not mean that there is agreement on the use of such a variable. Two particular aspects cause disagreement: definition and measurement. In both cases, authors have introduced new ideas to improve on the use of class as an explanatory variable. At the basic level, class is a way of describing different groups in society, the members of each sharing similar levels of such factors as income, lifestyle, status, life opportunity or power. Beyond that there is argument as to which of these factors needs to be included and how many divisions are important. Arguments over measurement centre both on the appropriateness of different statistical techniques and on what exactly is to be measured. After outlining the main aspects of disagreement in these two areas, the study of class voting is considered in terms of the effect the voting behaviour orthodoxy has on it.

Certain distinctions, such as working- or middle-class, blue- or white-collar, manual or non-manual, are generally accepted by all who use class schemata. But once further refinements are added, disagreements appear. Early works used the 'social grade' categories that the opinion polling companies use, with a small adjustment to divide the block of lower non-manual workers. These divisions are based on a basic manual/non-manual divide, but also take account of standard of living and lifestyle. The social grade categories are usually referred to by letters ranging from A to E, but Butler and Stokes (1974, p.72) used Roman numerals I to V instead. Sarlvik and Crewe continued with this schema for the sake of comparison (1983, p.75). But as the relationship between class and party, as traditionally measured, began to weaken, later authors started to refine the definitions of class by bringing in new dividing lines. Two examples illustrate the types of changes that were introduced. Dunleavy and Husbands (1985, p.122) added two further divisions: 'those who own some means of production and those who do not' and 'those whose work involves controlling other people's labour ... and those who are simply wage-earners'. Their new schema was designed to take account of 'location in a system of production and by the level of power that people can exert over their own work tasks' (p.121). Their model also looks at the importance of other work-related variables, such as trade union membership and if the employer is in the private or public sector. Heath and his colleagues also took account of people's 'supervisory functions or greater amount of discretion and autonomy' and of individuals' 'exposure to market forces' (Heath et al., 1985, p.16), as well as the traditional manual/non-manual divide. While the basic difference between using primarily physical and using primarily mental energy remains, other aspects of class definitions have changed. Even the hierarchical nature of the earlier schemata has been removed by Heath's team. Added to all of these academically defined definitions there is also the alternative of using self-perceived class by asking people if they think of themselves in class terms, and if so which one. In this case, answers are usually given using working-class/middle-class labels or some finer definition such as lower-middle-class.

Despite the claim that the alternative class schemata make only small differences and a factory worker will always be working-class and a teacher always middle-class (Rose and McAllister, 1986, p.35), some types of jobs will be classified differently under different schemata. Take a secretary who oversees four typists in a local, private company. Under the Heath et al. (1985) schema, a white-collar supervisor of others is 'salariat'. For Dunleavy and Husbands the private sector aspect is important, as is the supervisory role, and a secretary is 'non-manual'. Applying older classifications, our secretary is C1 (lower middle-class) in the 'market research social grade' or, 'III(N)' (skilled

non-manual) for the Registrar General list. However, if our secretary
is a woman, then earlier studies would have placed her in a class
according to her husband's job. If he is a foreman electrician for the
local council, he is skilled manual for both the market research and
Registrar General schemata (C2 and III(M) respectively). So if this same
woman had been regularly surveyed she would have been categorized
in four different ways (see Table 4.1) even though she never changed
her job. In broad terms, early working-class classifications would have
predicted a Labour vote and later, middle-class ones a Conservative
vote. But if we put our hypothetical pair into the Welsh constituency
of Caernarfon, then they are likely to vote Plaid Cymru.

Table 4.1 Changing class categories for a female secretary who oversees
four typists in a local, private company

Date	Classification system used	Code
1964 or 1974 BES	Butler and Stokes, for electrician husband	V (skilled manual)
1983 survey	Dunleavy and Husbands	Non-manual, private sector
1987 BES	Heath *et al.*	Salariat
1991 census	Registrar General	III(N) (skilled non-manual)

'Class' seems to be used as a compound variable that describes
and measures the aspects of a person's position which affect his or her
vote. Working-class people do not vote Labour just because of that
label, but because of what that label means to their life: it is an instrumental vote. Early definitions were based on lifestyle and income and
each party was seen as benefiting the members of a certain class.
Later definitions moved away from income hierarchies to bring in
aspects such as level of control over the work situation, union
membership, housing or education, as these factors are seen to relate
to the voting decision. There was still the idea of an instrumental
link: 'It is these differences ["market situation" and employment
conditions], not those of income, which determine the interests of the
different classes, their potential for political action and their sym-
pathies for rival political ideologies' (Heath *et al.*, 1985, p.16). The
term 'class' is maintained, but it is used to mean different things. While
class remains a measure of social location, it is redefined to bring in
new important factors in the voting decision. Factors become important as they are politicized, so changing politics needs changing class

definitions. Parties represent groups on either side of important dividing lines so 'what we need is a conception of social class that reveals
the social roots of dissensus' (Heath *et al.*, 1985, p.14). As politics and
society change so must the definition of class, but in so doing 'class'
becomes the label for all the factors relating to work that may affect
the vote, rather than any clearly defined universal term.

   Even when there is agreement on the way to define class,
arguments abound as to how to measure class voting. Again, the
original idea is simple: given class-based parties, the proportion
of people voting for the party associated with their class can be
quantified and used to compare levels across elections. Part of the
conceptual problem is that the level of class voting is not the only
thing that changes from one election to another. At any one time,
even when using a simple working-class/middle-class divide, the two
groups are not the same size and they have changed as work
patterns in Britain have changed (Heath *et al.*, 1985, p.30). A tenth of
working-class voters in 1964 would constitute a different number
of people from a tenth of middle-class voters in 1964 or a tenth of
working-class voters in 1994. Similarly, the share of the vote received
by each party at each election differs. Not only does a measure of
class voting have to quantify this phenomenon, but it must also
be unaffected by overall movements in the size of the classes or
party votes.

   A more important problem relates to the focus of interest. Is a
study of class-based voting looking at which party each class predominantly voted for or which class made up the biggest part of each
party's vote? The answers are not necessarily the same. For example,
in 1979, Labour was not the party of the working-class, but the
working-class was the class of the Labour party (Sarlvik and Crewe,
1983, p.88). This seeming paradox occurs because Labour's vote
came mainly from the working-class, but most of that class's vote did
not go to Labour. Usually, it is the share each party gains within a
class that is used: how class feeds into party rather than the reliance
of the party on each class. As with swing, there has been discussion of
the relevance of absolute or relative measures. Is it enough to look at
those who vote for their class party (absolute measures), or does the
level of other voting need to be considered too (relative measures)?
But within relative measures there is the problem of which type of
behaviour is considered as the opposite of class voting: cross-class
voting or non-class voting (Scarbrough, 1987, p.224). If there were
only two classes and two vote options that were each related to a

class, then this problem would not arise, as a non-class vote would be a cross-class vote. But increasingly authors deal with more than two classes and there have always been more than two voting options. Therefore, it is important to be clear about what aspects class voting is compared to. Various techniques have been used to try to take account of these conceptual problems.

Table 4.2 Calculations of class effect

1987 vote within salariat and working-class (out of a total of 2,860 voters)

	Salariat			Working-class		
	Number	% of class	% of voters	Number	% of class	% of voters
Conservative	470	56	16.4	317	31	11.1
Labour	126	15	4.4	491	48	17.2
Liberal Democrat	243	29	8.5	215	21	7.5

Calculations of class voting using 1987 data

Method	Calculation	Answer
Alford (Labour)	$48-15$	33
Absolute	$\frac{470 + 491}{2,860} \times 100$	33.6
Odds ratio	$\frac{(56 \div 15)}{(31 \div 48)}$	5.78
Scarbrough odds ratio	$\frac{(56 \div 44)}{(52 \div 48)}$	1.17
Index of Determination	$16.4 + 8.5^1 + 17.2$	42.1

[1] Assumes Liberals are salariat.
Values in top half of table are taken from Heath *et al.*, 1991, p.69.

Probably the best-known measure of class voting is the Alford Index, which subtracts the percentage of non-manual people voting Labour from the percentage of manual workers voting Labour (see Table 4.2). The more precise, but less frequently used, 'absolute class voting' measures the percentage of voters who voted for their class by adding the number of non-manual Conservative voters to the number of manual Labour voters and dividing by the total number of voters, multiplied by 100 (Denver, 1989, p.54). The Index of Determination, which adds the percentage of voters who vote for the party that theory says it should vote for (Rose and McAllister, 1986, p.38), is another type of absolute class measure that recognizes a wider range of parties. Relative class voting looks at the relative strength of each party in the different social classes (Heath *et al.*, 1991, p.64) by using the 'odds ratio'. First the odds of a person from one class voting Conservative rather than Labour are calculated for each class: the percentage of non-manual Conservative voters is divided by the percentage of non-manual Labour voters and the percentage of manual Conservative voters is divided by the percentage of manual Labour voters. Then the ratio of the two odds is found by dividing the non-manual figure by the manual figure.

While the descriptions of the different measures may look like torture by arithmetic, they each quantify a different aspect of class voting. Each technique singles out a particular part of the relationship between class and party and uses that to signify the whole, more complex, relationship. Not surprisingly, there are arguments over the relevance of the different measures and their ability to measure what they set out to measure. The introduction of each successive approach was a criticism of previous ones, each seeking to improve on the others. Dunleavy (1987) launched the strongest attack on the newest measure of odds ratios, both as a concept and a statistical technique (see Denver and Hands, 1992, section 2 for a summary of the arguments).

As has been shown, discussion of class voting gives a strong impression of great argument. However, while this debate is real, it is again taking place within the confines of the orthodoxy. Several familiar orthodox themes are apparent in the use of class: concentration on Labour and Conservative; vote as support; and the stress on over-time comparison. Although arguments relating to class are often perceived to be statistical in nature, it is the conceptual parts of the orthodoxy rather than methodology that have the greatest impact on this debate.

Common to both absolute and relative measures of class voting is a need for two classes and two parties and therefore concentration on Conservative and Labour. Early works felt safe in ignoring the Liberals because they were 'classless', drawing votes equally from across the classes (Butler and Stokes, 1974, p.79; Sarlvik and Crewe, 1983, p.79). Some later studies have refuted this idea, assigning Liberal voting to the 'salariat' (Heath *et al.*, 1985, p.21) and expressly recognizing a multi-party context (Heath *et al.*, 1991, p.69; Dunleavy and Husbands, 1985, Chapter 6; Johnston *et al.*, 1988, Chapter 4). However, multi-party analysis does not try to come up with a single measure of class voting. The analysis done by Heath and his colleagues looking at all parties and classes is much briefer and less often mentioned than the two-party odds ratio technique (Dunleavy, 1987, p.411). Measures of relative class voting are particularly prone to problems of what to do with third party votes. Scarbrough (1987, p.224) has argued that Heath and his colleagues should be looking at the 'non-class' vote rather than the 'cross-class' vote in their ratio. By using only Conservative and Labour votes, they count all third-party votes as cross-class votes, implying such voters always vote in the 'wrong' class. However, if all non-class votes were used together then third-party voters would be seen as outside the class/vote relationship (see Table 4.2).

While various authors mention the problem of third-party votes, they tend to ignore non-voters and differential abstention rates (one exception is Johnston *et al.*, 1988). If members of a class are turning to abstention then this affects overall levels of class voting: the parties are receiving smaller shares of the potential vote from that class. If one class sees an increase in non-voting not matched in other classes, then this will again have an effect on overall class voting levels, but will not be picked up by any of the measures used. Non-voting is an option at an election. The few studies that have considered non-voting (for example, Denver and Hands, 1985; Eagles and Erfle, 1989) suggest that community variables such as marginality or cohesion have a greater effect than individual factors. However, Denver and Hands (1985, p.383) did include class-related variables in their analysis. Non-voting varies across areas and elections and may affect election results, so should be studied as carefully as actual votes cast. Clearly, the orthodox concentration on just Labour and Conservative impacts on the usefulness of the different measures used.

Despite the many different definitions of class that are used, the orthodox assumption that a vote is a sign of support is apparent in the debate. Most of the changes in definition of class voting are designed to make aspects of class more relevant to the voting decision. Categories related to power within the work situation or exposure to the market or trade union membership are included because it is postulated that these will affect views on politics and the parties. There is an instrumental aspect to these assumptions: a vote is related to what the party can do for people within that group or class. Again, this approach rests on an assumption of vote as support.

Nothing is made of the possible emotional and traditional class antagonism or of the related aversion towards giving a vote to 'the other side'. Explanation concentrates on why members of that class should like the party they vote for, rather than any suggestion that they may be driven by a class-related dislike of another party. Early work looking at working-class Tories contained some mention of these aspects (for example, McKenzie and Silver, 1968, p.110), but later studies have concentrated on the positive, instrumental links between class and party voted for. As with the general neglect of negative voting discussed in Chapter 2, this concentration on class as having a positive impact on vote misses important aspects of voter behaviour.

Methodological aspects of the orthodox approach also affect studies of class voting. All the problems with survey questions that are used to elicit facts impact on the accurate measurement of class, especially, as has been noted by several authors (Denver, 1989, p.63; Dunleavy, 1987, p.409), when data collected for use in one schema are recategorized into another schema that is dependent on different variables. For instance, being self-employed makes a big difference in the classification used by Heath and his colleagues (1985, 1991) but not in the early studies that they recategorize. But the great emphasis placed on over-time comparison leads analysts into attempts at historical reclassification.

Questions about the direction of causality are rarely mentioned in studies of class voting. The assumption is always that class affects vote because class is established first and is less easy to choose than party. In general, class is determined by life chances rather than choice. But later, more complex definitions of class include aspects that are chosen by individuals. People choose to be self-employed rather than employed by others; they choose whether or not to join a union; they choose a public or private sector employer; they choose to become a supervisor. While some of these options are more forced than others, depending on the job market, individuals nevertheless have some ability to decide. It is these very differences that are demonstrated to have an effect: it was being self-employed or a supervisor that tended to conservatism (Heath *et al.*, 1985, p.20); unionized, public sector non-manual workers are particularly anti-Conservative (Dunleavy and Husbands, 1985, p.133). In a study of CND (Campaign for Nuclear Disarmament) activists, Parkin (1968, p.185) discusses the tendency of middle-class radicals to work in jobs with a welfare or creative base. The idea is one of causality that runs from views to job rather than vice versa; selection rather than recruitment. People may be making these job choices because of their existing political predisposition towards trade unions or power over their work situation or the public sector. For these people, the clear connection between class and political party is not necessarily an explanation, as both may derive from some other source of political outlook. Again the orthodox concentration on the vote as the variable to be explained affects the types of explanations that are considered.

The orthodoxy frames the debate over class voting in a number of ways. The orthodox interpretation that voters choose the best option and support the party they vote for, means that studies of class voting concentrate on positive links between class and party. Other possible links, such as distrust of another party, are sidelined. Vote options other than Conservative and Labour also suffer, again reflecting the orthodox acceptance of a two-party system. Consequently, only some types of class voting are debated. The main aspects of the orthodox methodology to affect class voting are the overriding desire for comparability over time and the strict focus on vote as the key variable to be explained. The need for comparability can lead to reclassification of respondents in old surveys, with less than perfect information. Consideration of the debate around class voting provides a clear example of how much disagreement can occur within the confines of an orthodox approach and methodology.

Context Effects

Unlike party identification and class voting, ideas of a context effect are not widely discussed in the mainstream literature. Here, the orthodoxy works to exclude or sideline an idea. While the early Michigan and Columbia works stressed the importance of group membership, this aspect seems to have been lost. In later works, the only type of personal contact regularly considered was that of the parent(s) and sometimes the spouse. In ideas of a context effect, sometimes called a 'neighbourhood effect', the social and physical context is seen as important. Information about the place in which a person lives is seen as relevant to attempts to understand that person's voting behaviour. Miller encapsulated the idea when he said, 'those who speak together vote together' (1977, p.65). Dunleavy, with equal eloquence, retorts that, 'we cannot simply assume that political alignment brushes off on people by rubbing shoulders in the street' (1979, p.413). As an individual's context or neighbourhood can cover many aspects, this concept is sometimes hard to pin down and measure.

Hints of some sort of context or neighbourhood effect can be gleaned from the core works. There is recognition that behaviour at election time differs in different constituencies (for example, Denver, 1989, p.96; Dunleavy and Husbands, 1985, p.189; Heath *et al.*, 1985, p.74), and that locality may alter the effects of other variables such as class (Johnston *et al.*, 1988, p.127). Following from Miller's (1977) work on the correlation between vote and socio-economic variables at the constituency level, there is some recognition that the class of an area has an effect as well as the individual's class. For instance, Johnston's team found that 'in general, it was the case that the more homogeneous a community, the more likely it was that members of all occupational classes would vote for the political party... with the strongest links to the largest class' (Johnston *et al.*, 1988, p.92). There definitely seems to be something out there, so 'the case for "class contagion" cannot then be dismissed. Although the evidence is largely circumstantial, it is not inconsiderable' (Scarbrough, 1987, p.239).

Having recognized some truth in Miller's assertion and accepted that there are local effects in voting, the troublesome question of how these can be explained arises. Dunleavy derides the idea of acquiring partisan feeling by osmosis, but a number of more practical suggestions for the transmission of a local feeling have been mooted. Putnam (1966, pp.640–1), in one of the earliest works on context effects, suggested three theoretical explanations for a neighbourhood effect: greater effort by the majority party; conforming to local norms; interaction. Little is said in works on voting behaviour about the first suggestion, although Lutz (1981, p.311) mentions the possible effect of seeing lots of posters for one party. Ideas of conforming to the local norm are also rarely mentioned, but other theories relating to an awareness of the locality are present. Some suggest that voters look to the good of the community rather than themselves: 'To the extent that people in areas of high unemployment (and not just the unemployed themselves) blame the incumbent government for the situation, so they are likely to vote against it' (Johnston *et al.*, 1988, p.165). Or, more cautiously: 'Certainly, it is clear that *individual* differences in income, unemployment and so on cannot explain the regional differences in voting behaviour. Perceptions of the *community's* economic situation might therefore provide the answer' [italics from original] (Heath *et al.*, 1991, p.112). The local, rather than national, economic situation may be crucial in assessments of the success of the government (Owens and Wade, 1988, p.50). The suggestion is that variation in the economic health of different areas of Britain and voters' awareness of this situation may account for spatial variations in the vote.

Other models concentrate on the 'ghetto' aspects of locality. Differing patterns of occupation, income, age or housing (McAllister and Studlar, 1992) or concentrations of the 'core classes' (Miller, 1978, p.258) may account for the spatial differences in voting behaviour. Central to this approach is the idea that areas of similar housing will attract people who share other important variables, such as income or job type. In effect, 'the line between a council house estate and owner-occupiers' residences is a recognised social boundary between neighbourhoods, and differences in architecture, shopping patterns and road and bus routes reinforce these distinctions' (Rose and McAllister, 1986, p.60). It may be that the political views are not acquired from the neighbourhood, but that a political predisposition plays a part in the choice of where to live. So the middle-class Labour voter may choose to live in a more working-class area because of Labour views (Harrop and Miller, 1987, p.210), and thus the direction of causality between housing type and political views cannot be ascertained using present datasets (Heath *et al.*, 1991, p.122). However, one case study found this explanation wanting (Eagles, 1992, p.239). Functional variables, such as housing, account for spatial voting, and discernible physical or socio-economic boundaries, such as housing estates, separate neighbourhoods in these models.

Interaction as the crucial aspect of a context effect is central to several works. However, there are different ideas about how such contacts affect partisan views. Butler and Stokes (1974, p.150) suggested that some voters relied on local types of information, but Bodman (1983) was not able to substantiate their model. The crucial role of various groups acting as mediators is mentioned in several studies (for example, Fitton, 1973; MacKuen and Brown, 1987; Miller, 1978; Putnam, 1966). Individual membership of any type of local group, whether organized or based on social contacts, provides an identity or focus for political views. A form of local 'socialization' whereby newcomers learn to fit in with the dominant group is also suggested (Fitton, 1973; Putnam, 1966). Common to all these ideas is the importance of actual contact between people within the 'neighbourhood': 'contact operates through interactions with identifiable friends and neighbours: concrete personal relations rather than amorphous community norms are the proximate cause' (MacKuen and Brown, 1987, p.484). The community or neighbourhood, therefore, describes a network of personal contacts rather than a geographical area. It is close contact with other people in the neighbourhood that affects political views.

Alongside debate on the way in which a context effect operates, is some discussion of when local factors may be relevant. Consistently, the locality is seen as being just one of a variety of factors influencing the voting decision, acting to moderate or reinforce other variables, such as class or education. However, local factors may have a greater influence when partisanship is weak. Individuals may be particularly prone to a 'neighbourhood effect' when they are in a state of flux. Several of the studies showed that newcomers were particularly prone to changing their views or partisanship to match the new milieu (Lutz, 1986, p.456; Putnam, 1966, p.652). Similarly, local views may have more impact on the specifics of current issues than on deep-rooted attitudes and beliefs. Thus the impact of a context effect may differ according to the issue (MacKuen and Brown, 1987, p.485). Most work on a context effect concentrates on voting, but it may be more appropriate to concentrate on specific assessments of issues and parties.

While mentions of some kind of neighbourhood or context effect are fairly common in the core texts, detailed analysis of the phenomenon is not. In a recent compendium of pieces covering *Issues and Controversies in British Electoral Behaviour* (Denver and Hands, 1992) there is no section on context or neighbourhood effects. Within the mainstream texts on voting behaviour the effect of locality is not given great weight, but it remains an unsolved problem. The question, then, is why this group of factors which may affect partisan views and voting has been largely ignored. Discussing the absence of a factor is more difficult than examining the treatment of an included factor. If something is excluded, by definition, little will be said about it. Therefore, looking at the orthodox (non)treatment of a context effect entails some reading between the lines. In doing this, those aspects of the orthodox approach and method that tend to lead away from analysis of a context effect may be unearthed.

Some of the basic assumptions about voting behaviour contained in the orthodox approach have helped to sideline the study of a neighbourhood effect in the major psephological works. This is one instance where Butler and Stokes cannot be blamed for their drawing of the boundaries of research. Rather, some of the basic assumptions central to the orthodox approach preclude any idea of local variation caused by some sort of neighbourhood effect. In particular, ideas that the voting decision is one of deciding which option is best and an unquestioning acceptance of system factors, can be seen to help exclude this variable.

Early work looking at specific localities found that debate of political issues with those who held different views was minimal (Berelson *et al.*, 1954, p.106) and change unusual. Hence, the focus of attention moved from individual change to widespread stability. The move from the Columbia to the Michigan model, as outlined in Chapter 1, is largely responsible for the marginalization of the study of a neighbourhood effect. Butler and Stokes (1974, pp.130–7) did cover local factors such as class and religious composition, but this was not seen by others as part of their core model. Dunleavy and Husbands are alone in mentioning the 'local class environment' (1985, p.6). Central to the basic party identification model is the idea of learnt partisanship, so group identity does play a part. The crucial group was defined as class rather than neighbourhood. But, as Miller suggests, the decisive collective view may depend less on 'people like me' and more on 'people around here' (1978, p.283). The linear nature of development from *Political Change in Britain* (Butler and Stokes, 1969, 1974) has helped to draw attention towards fierce fights over class definition and away from other kinds of group identity. Job rather than locality has been seen as defining political position and interest.

The orthodox interpretation sees the voting decision as primarily a choice of what is best for the voter. While there is some recognition that 'best' may be viewed in class terms (Butler and Stokes, 1974, Chapter 4), the idea is not expanded to incorporate other group interests. If the idea of a local effect caused by an awareness of the local economic or political situation is accepted, then a different idea of 'best' is implied. Voters may still be considering their own economic wellbeing, but using local rather than national indicators as a guide to the likelihood of future prosperity. Models that see the neighbourhood as a reference group for individuals also provide alternative suggestions about what is 'best', this time with a more general reference to the important local group. When group identity, however defined, is strong, then what is best for the group will be seen by individuals as best for them. The problem is in determining which group the individual uses as a reference for assessing the political parties on offer.

The orthodox non-questioning of system biases such as the framework created by the way in which elections operate may also
impinge on the study of a neighbourhood effect. Votes are counted in
a constituency, and so that unit of measure is used to analyse
patterns of voting. The constituency is the smallest unit for which we
have voting statistics. Votes are not counted separately for each
polling booth, as they are in some other places, such as New Zealand,
so we cannot know how voters in different areas within a constituency voted. Although census data are available for smaller units, the
corresponding general election voting statistics are not. Hence a
community of a meaningful size, within a constituency, cannot be
studied using published data. Analysis that does consider the possible
effect of local factors tends to accept the constituency as a valid unit.
It is a constituency, not a smaller unit, that has an incumbent MP
or a marginal result or a woman MP or a three-way contest or a
Liberal candidate. Those analysing such factors have to do so at the
constituency level (for example, Dunleavy and Husbands, 1985,
pp.204–11). In the same way, the presence of the first-past-the-post
voting system and thus the importance of who receives the most
votes in a constituency are accepted rather than questioned. The
effect of marginality, for example, is considered for a constituency
rather than a smaller or wider area. However, there have been
some indications that local effects can spill over into neighbouring
constituencies. For instance, in the 1987 election, the strong Labour
vote in Liverpool rippled out to produce higher than expected Labour
votes in surrounding areas (Butler and Kavanagh, 1988, p.329).

Methodological aspects of the orthodox approach are the most
easily detectable in explanations for the scarcity of discussion of a
neighbourhood effect. The British Election Survey was established as
a national survey designed to provide information about the country
as a whole. A sample that covered the entire country and at the
same time allowed for sufficient respondents within each locality to
enable neighbourhood analysis would be vast. In the 1987 sample,
24 names were taken from each of 250 constituencies to give 6,000
potential respondents, but at least eight times as many names would
be needed to give any chance of locality-based analysis. When
samples from a succession of elections are added together, the possibility of analysing local groups is there, but then there is the problem
of a changed political context. Just because voters lived in the same
constituency in 1974, 1979 and 1983 does not mean that they had
the same context. The MP may change and so too can marginality,

unemployment levels or the mix of housing types. Even when survey data are aggregated into smaller groups, the difficulties of defining a real community come into play, so again measurements may not really gauge the concept under investigation. The desire to investigate local effects is not compatible with the needs of a national survey.

A constituency and a community are not the same thing, the latter in most cases being far smaller than the former. However, much analysis of context effects uses the constituency as the basic local unit (for example, McAllister and Studlar, 1992, p.186; Bodman, 1983, p.249). Although related to geographical analysis, a 'community' need not even constitute all who live in a given area. There is no real agreement on what constitutes a community in a way that has relevance for the idea of a neighbourhood effect. The neighbourhood may be the area 'within walking distance' of the house (Rose and McAllister, 1986, p.60), or a network of friendships and contacts (Fitton, 1973, p.456). The relevant community may well vary in size from person to person (Putnam, 1966, p.641). Rather than prescribe some definition of neighbourhood, and thus the relevant area of political influence, it may be necessary to ask individuals whom they associate with. Fitton (1973) used three small streets for his analysis, and asked people whom they talk to, so building up a picture of the actual networks. Similarly, MacKuen and Brown (1987) asked survey respondents for their perception of their neighbours' partisanship and change in view. 'Contagion' only works when there is interaction or the local view has saliency for the individual, so people have to be asked to identify their relevant 'neighbourhood'. The current methods for collecting data mean that the constituency is often substituted for the community. Sufficient information on smaller areas is not available and even if it were, we do not necessarily have the information to determine correctly the extent of a relevant neighbourhood.

Relevant questions on local effects are absent from the traditional range of survey questions. In particular, they have not included 'social network' or 'friendship' measures (Scarbrough, 1987, p.239) or asked for assessments of the local situation. While some case studies of particular neighbourhoods have been conducted (for example, Fitton, 1973; Eagles, 1992), neighbourhood factors still remain outside the major election studies. Conventional survey questionnaires do not include questions that provide information about the local rather than the national situation. Work using aggregate data to look at context effects also faces problems of which measures to use. Taking account of socio-economic factors depends on the use of appropriate variables, such as housing or class. However, Miller (1978) found that 'percentage professional and managerial' was a better predictor than more common class categories. Relevant aggregate measures have to both tap the essence of the concept and be easily available for the appropriate unit. It may be that different factors are more important in different areas or for different neighbourhoods (Rasmussen, 1973, p.142). Present practices in the collection of data, both survey and aggregate, hinder the study of a neighbourhood effect.

The orthodoxy plays a major role in sidelining discussion of the neighbourhood effect in British voting behaviour. The concentration on nationwide surveys to discover general trends makes it difficult to look at local factors, and the tendency to ignore the way in which the electoral system and party system work to create different local contests also plays a role. A study looking for general trends assumes that the people across the country experienced the same election, but actually a first-past-the-post election is a whole series of local competitions held on the same day. While the national campaigns run by the political parties are seen across the country, the local campaigns differ. Each area will also be unique in terms of which parties are contesting the seat and how well they have done in the past.

Summary

Arguments about party identification, class voting and a context effect vary in content and intensity, but all are affected by the orthodoxy. Other areas of debate within the study of voting behaviour are also affected in various ways by the orthodox approach, but these three are good examples of the form the effects take. The accepted boundaries of debate help to contain arguments over partisanship and class voting and to sideline discussion of a neighbourhood effect. Both the conceptual aspects and assumptions central to the orthodox approach and the orthodox methodology play a part in moulding these three arguments.

The overriding desire for continuity in questionnaire design is a feature of the way in which all three debates have developed. An emphasis on comparability has given great weight to the measures established by Butler and Stokes. The early decision to exclude a non-identification option in the basic party identification question has been continued despite suggestions that this overestimates the extent of partisanship. Similarly, the omission of a section of questions on local contacts and perceptions of the neighbourhood has been followed. The perceived need for continuity makes the inclusion of new banks of questions difficult. Questions needed for the class categorizations have expanded, but there is still a desire to provide measures that can be used for longitudinal comparisons. Traditional questionnaire design has played a part in the debate over these three crucial areas. The establishment of the election survey as one based on a national, random sample has also contributed to the difficulty of exploring neighbourhood effects, because such a study needs a more localized sample.

Orthodox adherence to the idea that a vote can be decoded as a sign of support plays a central role in the debates examined here. Assessment of levels of class-based voting rests on the idea that there is a positive link between class and party. Because a vote is seen as a sign of support, negative class effects or links are not examined, which affects the kinds of measures that are used. Similarly, the related idea that the voting decision is the choice of the party that is 'best', centres analysis on individual rather than locality based explanations. People are deemed to make choices in relation to personal characteristics, such as age or class, rather than in relation to the local situation. In this way, a neighbourhood effect is pushed to the periphery. The relations between current concepts of party identification and the idea of a vote as a sign of support are more complex and interconnected. British accounts of party identification have lost the acceptance of voting deviance that is central to the American model. Therefore, the vote is seen as a manifestation of partisanship and thus read as a sign of long-standing support. But this connection is taken as applying universally and not just to partisans, and so helps to create the orthodox idea of vote as support.

The orthodox acceptance of system biases or effects also plays its part in these debates. The normal concentration on Labour and the Conservatives helps to shape the standard way in which class is discussed. By focusing on the two major parties a clear dichotomy can be used, but at the expense of studying the growing number of 'minor party' voters. Limits imposed by existing constituency boundaries play a part in the problems of studying a neighbourhood effect. And the first-past-the-post voting system shapes the characteristics of constituencies that are then used to look at variations in voting behaviour. There is a tendency for these system effects to be accepted as part of the framework, rather than investigated as part of the possible range of influences on the vote.

This chapter has detailed three areas of voting behaviour where argument abounds. Showing how the orthodoxy frames these debates illustrates the power of the normative approach and methodology. Again the habitual decoding of a vote as a sign of support is important, as is the desire for continuity of questions in the core surveys. The orthodoxy provides a strong framework that can make some aspects difficult to study and shape the form of debate in other areas. Although the study of voting behaviour enjoys fierce debate, such arguments are still conducted within the framework of the orthodoxy.

5

Alternatives to the Orthodoxy

Having spent four chapters outlining and criticizing the orthodoxy, I feel it is time to consider some alternatives. The orthodox approach covers three key elements, namely the aims of voting behaviour studies, key aspects of interpretation and ideas of what should be covered. The orthodox methodology affects the collection and use of data. Concentration on the use of attitudinal survey data to look at national trends to explain the differing levels of vote received by each major party is common to both approach and methodology. In interpreting the data, there is a basic assumption that voters choose what they see as the 'best' option and so each vote is a sign of support for that party. The normative area of study routinely excludes certain groups, such as minor party voters, and types of behaviour, such as a tactical vote, and possible context effects like the working of the first-past-the-post electoral system. In other words analysis concentrates on what is seen as the typical voter. In the area of methodology, studies looking at possible problems with surveys are routinely ignored. Taken together, the orthodox approach and methodology have channelled the study of voting behaviour in Britain down one road. This chapter considers other avenues or byways that could be taken.

Not all that has been written on voting behaviour is contained within the orthodoxy, although the main British texts are included here. It is useful to look at those works which have taken a different path to see what they did. The British orthodoxy is centred in the Anglo-American arena; voting behaviour studies from other countries may indicate alternative avenues. The orthodoxy is embedded in the political science discipline, but other disciplines may have useful methods from which to borrow. The first section of this chapter covers aspects of these 'other' approaches, while the second section discusses ways in which voting behaviour studies in Britain could develop so as to meet some of the criticisms made of the orthodox way.

'Other' Approaches

The study of elections is widespread, but the studies vary in terms of the available data and the focus of the analysis. While elections are commonplace, not all countries have regular election surveys. For instance, there has never been a national election survey in the Republic of Ireland. Therefore, the study of individual attitudes and voting behaviour cannot be carried out in all democracies. Where surveys are conducted, there are many similarities of approach. In particular, existing survey questions are borrowed and replicated. In many countries, it is possible to trace an evolution of survey-based electoral studies similar to the one described for Britain in Chapter 1. Discussion of party identification and the importance of socio-economic groupings such as class are common. Throughout, there is a dominance of ideas from the Michigan school. Many of the national election surveys that were set up in other countries relied heavily on the questionnaire designed by the Michigan team and involved academics who had spent some time at the Michigan Institute for Social Research. Academic study is not confined by nation state boundaries and there is wide circulation of ideas. However, there are some language boundaries, so that work reported in languages other than English only reaches Anglo-American academic circles when it is translated. Even so there is a vast available literature on voting behaviour, and the following survey gives some idea of the range in coverage.

Party identification remains strong in the Australian literature, although the 'new politics' of environmentalism and a concern for the quality of life are important new factors (Bean *et al.*, 1990). Writings on party identification and the Michigan model are still popular in the USA (for discussion of recent works see Pomper, 1988, Chapter 7). However, with declining levels of strong partisanship there has been some reassessment of those who say they are 'independent'. In particular, the use of survey questions asking which party the independents feel closer to have been popular. The main competition to this model comes from ideas of economic voting. Based on the concept of the individual as a rational utility maximizer, taken from economics, such studies tend to concentrate on issues and economic conditions (for example, Fiorina, 1981). Within the economic voting school there is much debate about the type of issues that voters consider when assessing the contenders. For instance, are voters making a retrospective or prospective judgement: commenting on what the government has done or choosing between promised policies? Related arguments look at whether voters focus on details of policy debates or on the outcomes of implemented policy. While there is much discussion between writers within each of the models, the major debate is between the two, and centres around the desirability of concentrating on continuity or change.

Socio-economic variables such as class or religion have been central to voting behaviour analysis in many countries. Studies in the Federal Republic of Germany have created new wide class groups based on lifestyle and including voter placement on attitude scales (Jesse, 1990, p.92). Voter placement within a matrix created by the three cross-cutting cleavages of class, culture and geography has traditionally shaped Norwegian voting behaviour studies (Listhaug, 1989, p.29). While class has never been a strong predictor of vote choice in Canada, the socio-economic groupings based on region and religion have been important (Gidengil, 1992). Grunberg (1988) details the recent debate in France about the direction of 'electoral sociology'. Stable political behaviour had fostered a concentration on sociological models looking at links between parties and key groups, such as class. However, recent changes in the political and party system have led to some reassessment of this stability-centred model. In the Netherlands, studies have traditionally concentrated on the stable links between parties and groups identified by religion, class and ideology. It is only since 1986, when the dominant Christian Democrat party started discussing possible coalition partners, that a study of voting behaviour related to the economic situation or policy specifics has become relevant (Middendorp and Tanke, 1990).

Much that is written about voting behaviour outside Britain follows similar paths and therefore does not offer an alternative to the orthodoxy. However, there are a growing number of studies and articles that do address different issues. The rest of this section briefly mentions some of those studies reported in English that in some way look at areas outside of the orthodox approach. Not all of these studies are by political scientists, but they do reveal evidence that is useful to understanding voters. For instance, work in cognitive psychology which covers the way in which people make decisions is included where the work has relevance to the voting decision.

Several studies have returned to the Columbia approach by looking at details of attitudes during the campaign period and examining the meaning of group attachment. Miller headed a team that conducted a rolling panel survey of the campaign and vote in the 1987 British election with a focus on how electors saw the process (Miller *et al.*, 1990). They studied the volatility of voters during that time and found that it was useful to distinguish between partisans and leaners when looking at campaign effects. Partisans are those who, when asked the basic party identification question, said that they identify with a party, and leaners are those who said that while they did not identify with a party, they did feel closer to one. During the long campaign from spring 1986 through to May 1987, issue motivations were important in helping voters reach a decision on how to vote, but tactical considerations took over during the official or short campaign that ran between the announcement of the election and polling day. The 1987 Canadian national election survey followed a similar design to allow for a study of attitude change and formation during the campaign period (Johnston *et al.*, 1992). The researchers wanted to look at the way in which the electoral choice was created by the parties, as well as how voters decided. Tracking both the party actions and voter attitudes during the campaign, they were able to look at how party strategists reacted to events and what effect this had on voters' perceptions. Both studies found that voters were aware of a strategic situation and that their expectations about the result affected their vote decision. In considering behaviour changes in the run up to the election, and asking for perceptions of the situation, these studies place themselves outside of the orthodoxy.

Voters' behaviour across different types of elections has increasingly come under scrutiny. In America, there is much talk about the number of people who, for example, vote for the Republican Presidential candidate and a Democrat in the Congressional contest. The study of such 'inconsistent' behaviour when faced with a series of elections for different offices, often called split-ticket voting, has produced some interesting results. Studies tend to be in federal countries, such as Australia, Canada and the United States, where both state and national governments make substantial decisions (for example, Beck *et al.*, 1992; Bowler and Denemark, 1993; Bowler, 1990a; McAllister and Darcy, 1992). Explanations for the differences range from voters' perceptions that there are different political systems operating (Blake, 1982), to the ways in which the electoral rules help to foster such behaviour (McAllister and Darcy, 1992). Beck and colleagues (1992), in their study of votes for five state office holders in Ohio, found that voter attitude, in the form of partisanship, and system effects, in terms of the visibility of the candidates, were the two biggest influences on split voting. Bowler (1990a) changed the focus slightly and looked at split party identification in Canada. That is, people who say they identify with one party in the context of a general election and another party when the elections to provincial legislatures are discussed. He suggests that attitudes or behaviour at the different electoral levels should be studied in tandem, because they affect each other.

Patterns of voting across other groups of ballots are also of interest. Grunberg (1988) reports on work by Parodi looking at different behaviour in local, national and European elections in France – for example, a voter who votes for the socialist candidate in national and Presidential elections and for the communist in local elections. He suggests that French voters see local and European elections as a safe place to protest or support more extreme parties, because the control of national government is not at issue. Jesse (1988) looks at a different kind of split voting in the Federal Republic of Germany. The voting system there asked for a separate vote for the local MP and for a party list. Although most people gave their two votes to the same party, some did not. Minor parties are frequently the recipient of part of a split vote in Germany, suggesting that voters recognize the tactical situation and the different ways in which the two votes are used to create the legislature. Studies of nineteenth-century voting in Britain look at similar patterns of splitting multiple votes. Prior to the introduction of the secret ballot in 1872, details of how each person voted were recorded and some of these pollbooks are still intact. Therefore, in the two-member constituencies where voters had two votes, patterns can be examined (for example, Drake, 1971; Cox, 1986). Many people gave both votes to the two candidates from the same party. Some voters opted for only one candidate and did not use their second vote, while others split their votes between the parties. The study of inconsistent voters; looking at reactions to different types of ballots; and not looking just at the vote in a general election, break from the orthodox concentration on a general election and consistent voters.

Some studies divide voters into groups that are not related to the party they voted for. They are looking at groups of people who behave in the same way, rather than all voters for one party. In a study of the way preferences are given in the elections in the

Republic of Ireland, Bowler and Farrell (1991) constructed five
types of preference patterns. 'Pure' voters give their preferences to
the candidates from one party then move on to the candidates for
another party, while the 'unravelling' voters vote for all of the
candidates from one party and then move across parties with their
remaining preferences. Levels of loyalty, as shown by voting for the
same party in consecutive preferences, formed the central aspect
of their typology. Granberg and Holmberg (1991) used panel data
from Sweden and the United States to look at the consistency
between what voters said they would do during the campaign and
what they did on election day. They identify five types of people
ranging from the stable, who vote for the party they said they
preferred, through recruits, who vote despite saying they had no
preference, to the unmobilized, who indicate no preference during
the campaign and do not vote. In their study of split-ticket voting in
Australia, Bowler and Denemark (1993) divided voters into splitters
and non-splitters. In each study the groups were then analysed
using socio-economic variables to look for effects of age, education
and so on, on the different behavioural types. In the orthodoxy,
the party voted for is the important variable to explain, so this con-
struction of new categories is a change from the norm.

Taking account of the specific political context features in a
number of studies. Grunberg (1988) reports on work by Lancelot,
suggesting that in France the political context or 'electoral supply'
must be given greater attention, because changing party allegiances
and the emergence of new parties have altered the choices offered
to voters and thus their behaviour. To understand what happens at
elections, we need to look at why new issues, such as immigration
or environmentalism, emerge and why new parties are created.
Bowler (1990b) investigates the interaction between party and
voter behaviour by focusing on the tolerance that voters have for a
change in a party's policy position. Powell and Whitten (1993)
found that differences in the degree to which voters can detect
which party within the coalition government was to blame, affected
the extent to which economic performance variables impacted on
vote choice. Various works looking at sophisticated voting include
variables on the specific political context in the constituency. In a
study of voting in USA Presidential primaries, voters were found to
weigh perceptions of the chance each candidate had of winning
with their feelings for the person (Abramson et al., 1992). The past
behaviour of voters and parties creates a distinct electoral frame-

work in each area, and it is in this context that voters make their decision at any given election. In this way it is important to realize that constituencies are social constructs, not neutral reference points (Cornford *et al.*, 1995). Two voters in the same constituency may perceive the electoral context in different ways. Similarly, the context in a constituency at one election will not be the same as it was in any previous election. So a vote decision is 'the interaction between the individual level attitudes ... and the incentive structure provided by the electoral system' (Bowler and Lanoue, 1992, p.485). In considering the specific context for each voter, these studies are a far remove from the orthodox method of finding general trends across the country.

Although social psychology was an important aspect of the Michigan approach, there seems to be more that could be taken from this discipline. Even a cursory reading of an introductory social psychology text (for example, Baron and Byrne, 1984) reveals a number of areas of research that might benefit the study of voting behaviour. Of particular interest are ideas relating to the way in which attitudes are created and decisions made. Work on attitude formation looks at the ways in which different pieces of information are used to build up an overall picture. The weighted average model suggests that all information is weighted and taken together to form an overall attitude. Research has shown that more weight is given to information gained through experience, arguments in line with one's own views, extreme or negative views and attributes related to people as opposed to objects.

These ideas could easily be applied to the way in which voters see parties and candidates in an election. The importance of experience could affect the impact of certain policies, for example, the differ-ence in views on the health service between a person who has recently had an operation and one who has not. The impact of negative and extreme views is relevant in light of the increasing use of negative and 'shock-tactic' advertising during the election campaign. Zaller and Feldman (1992) addressed the problem of voters seeming to have inconsistent views when they were asked for an opinion on the same issue in a number of surveys conducted over time. They suggest that most people do not have a set view on every issue, but instead react to a survey by retrieving accessible thoughts on the issue and then choosing an option. Which aspects are salient at the time of being questioned will be affected by what they have been thinking of recently and therefore how much they discuss politics.

The role of emotions in decision-making could also play an important part in understanding voting behaviour. Marcus and MacKuen (1993) looked at the effects of anxiety and enthusiasm on the way people assess information and thus form opinions and make decisions. Feelings of anxiety make people stop what they are doing and reconsider the situation; for example, anxiety about crime levels may cause voters to consider current information on the parties rather than relying on habit. So there is a likely effect of negative campaigning triggering more issue assessment rather than loyal voting. Enthusiasm, on the other hand, leads to a desire to have more involvement, such as voting, discussing politics or working in the campaign. Thus the type of emotion stirred up by the campaign will affect the kind of information that is used and how voters view the voting choice: 'Because individual voters thus act differently under different conditions, we can expect that the quality of the entire electorate's behaviour will vary when the macropolitical scene offers different blends of anxiety and enthusiasm' (Marcus and MacKuen, 1993, p.681). Bowler and Lanoue (1992) also suggest that the way voters feel about the parties will affect the way in which they approach the voting situation. In a study of tactical voting they found that voters with strong feelings of loyalty were less likely to consider a tactical vote, even in very marginal constituencies.

People use a variety of cues in the processing of information, such as stereotypes related to labels like the party or groups associated with the person. If voters know that a candidate is from the Greens, they will make assumptions about that person based on their stereotype of what a Green candidate will do and they may even use such views to 'correct' more specific information about the candidate (Rahn, 1993). In the same way, voters who feel favourably towards trade unions will attach that feeling to a candidate who is associated with a union, but those who dislike unions will tend to have negative views of the candidate (Miller et al., 1991). However, in looking at the effect of group membership on the vote, as many studies inside the orthodoxy do, it is important to consider the perception of the voter. Just because someone is in a group does not mean that he or she identifies with it, so it is important 'to distinguish the treatment of groups as social psychological categories from the use of groups as demographic descriptors' (Miller and Wlezien,

1993, p.6). Again the way that each voter perceives the situation is crucial. These ideas can be related back to ideas of the local context or neighbourhood effect on voting (see Chapter 4). The groups that you belong to and identify with are also likely to be the ones that provide opportunities for political discussion: 'individual voters are the constituent elements, but the constituent individuals are tied together in politically significant ways' (Huckfeldt and Sprague, 1991, p.157). Relevant groups are constructed by voters and each will differ. So just as three voters in the same place may construe the political situation differently, so too are they likely to have different views about which groups are relevant to their political views. Attitudes about candidates and parties are central to elections, so the vast cognitive psychology literature on attitude formation and decision making seems to have much to offer the study of voting behaviour. One clear lesson seems to be the need to look at how each individual perceives the situation rather than assuming a uniform view.

A New Approach

Much of the previous discussion of problems with the orthodoxy centred on aspects of voting behaviour that were not covered, such as tactical voting, and unstated assumptions about voters, such as the idea that a vote is a sign of support for the party. The question remains as to how voting behaviour can be modelled and understood in a way that includes such behaviour. What follows is a set of ideas as to how the study of voting behaviour in Britain could be widened to include the range of behaviour types that are seen. There is no data analysis to substantiate these ideas, because they rely on variables that have not hitherto been asked about in election surveys. These ideas build on the discussion of the orthodoxy and arguments about the effect this approach has had on the study of voting behaviour. Criticisms relating to two aspects of the orthodox approach are central to the proposed new focus: the normal interpretation that voters are choosing the best option, so a vote is a sign of support; and the tendency not to discuss the effects of the political system. Part of the problem with the orthodoxy is that the only line of questioning that it follows is 'why does each party get that number of votes?' This approach leaves many areas and groups out of the analysis and seeks to answer only part of the total puzzle. While the literature suggests a concentration on voting behaviour, the question is not as simple as that. The actual decision under scrutiny is who or what to vote for. In other words, which candidate in that time and place is preferred. But the orthodox assumption is that the decision being studied is which party to support. The detailed difference between 'preference' and 'support' is conceptually and analytically important (see Chapter 2). Preferences that are not based on a desire to support are not really considered in the orthodox literature and so must be included in any new approach. Aspects of the party and electoral systems affect the political context at an election and shape the type of decision open to voters. Therefore a wider focus for the study of voting behaviour needs to include information on the political system and on the way in which choices are both presented to voters and perceived by them. The proposed widened focus attempts to put voters into context and consider elections from the voter's perspective, rather than looking down on a homogeneous mass to seek general trends.

Determining what voters decide

To understand how voters decide which party to vote for we must first know how they view the voting decision. Orthodox studies of voting behaviour generally see the party voted for as the primary variable to be explained: they seek to reveal how Conservative voters at a specific general election differ from Labour voters. This approach assumes that the party voted for is the major factor that distinguishes between significant groups of voters. However, the prior difference that has to be examined is what type of decision voters think they are making. The orthodoxy assumes that voters choose the party they like best and then signal support through voting. Tactical and protest voting provide evidence of voters viewing the voting decision in different ways. In both cases voters are motivated by the desire to hurt a party they dislike, rather than by a desire to help a party that they like. So the important information in understanding these votes is knowing which party arouses feelings of aversion, because the identity of the party voted for is of secondary importance to the voter. In tactical voting the other key component in the decision is a wish to use the vote to affect the result, in other words to participate in selecting a winner (Catt, 1989, p.549). Here, the voter not only wants to avoid voting for a disliked party, but also wishes to take the necessary action to prevent its victory. So using a measure of relative feeling for the range of parties and another tapping the extent of a predominant desire to select a winner will provide information on how voters approach the voting decision. In concentrating on determining what it is that voters decide, motivational rather than partisan differences can be emphasized.

A measure of relative party feeling taps the extent to which voters have a clear preference ordering, the dominance of positive or negative feelings and the strength of such feelings. To create this measure each voter has to rate each party on a scale that includes both positive and negative ends. Combining responses from these scales produces a pattern that shows the relative feeling for all parties and can be used in a variety of ways. Looking at the extremes shows the balance between positive and negative feelings towards the political parties, which is important because it will affect the focus of attention in the voting decision (see Table 5.1). Positive partisans have stronger feelings in favour of one party than they do against another, while for negative partisans their strongest feeling is opposition to a party. For example, Wendy and Leon both prefer the Conservatives to all other parties, but Wendy is a positive partisan because she strongly likes the Conservatives, dislikes Labour and either likes or is neutral towards all other parties, while Leon is a negative partisan because he strongly dislikes Labour and likes the Conservatives. Similarly, Simon is a positive partisan because he has stronger positive than negative feelings: he strongly likes the Liberal Democrats, is neutral to Labour and the Greens and dislikes the Conservatives. Ali has a strong dislike for the Liberal

Table 5.1 Examples of relative party feeling

Name used in example	Strongly like	Like	Neutral	Dislike	Strongly dislike	Relative party feeling
Simon	LD		GR, LAB	CON		Positive partisan
Rachel	GR	LAB	LD	CON		Positive partisan
Wendy	CON	GR	LD	LAB		Positive partisan
Leon		CON		LD, GR	LAB	Negative partisan
Ali		GR		CON, LAB	LD	Negative partisan
Colleen			LAB, GR	LD	CON	Negative partisan
Pat	LAB		GR, LD		CON	Polarized
Joe		CON	LD	LAB, GR		Polarized

Key: CON = Conservative; GR = Green party; LAB = Labour; LD = Liberal Democrats

Democrats that is not balanced with a strong liking of any party, so he is a negative partisan. For polarized voters, a liking for one party is balanced with equal dislike for another: Pat strongly likes Labour, strongly dislikes the Conservatives and has neutral feelings about all other parties. In the same vein, Joe's liking for the Conservatives is balanced by a dislike for Labour and the Greens.

Voters in these three groups will approach the election in different ways. Those motivated by positive feelings towards a party would be exemplified by the classic party identifiers, while those whose feelings against a party are stronger would be more suscept-ible to strategic considerations. Polarized or neutral voters may see the voting decision in non-partisan terms, for example, concentrat-ing on issues or personalities. This group may also be more open to the influence of the campaign, and open to being persuaded into being a positive or negative partisan on election day. Recognizing negative as well as positive views of the parties and taking the way voters feel about the range of parties presented on the ballot paper into consideration widens the study of voter motivation to encapsulate more of the real decision scenario.

The voting choice can be seen either as a time to help select the winner or as an opportunity to express a preference for a party. While the action taken in each case may be the same, the crucial difference is in the perceived audience. Expressive voters are prim-arily voting to make a point, to signal what they believe in, to stand up and be counted. A lifelong Labour voter who automatically votes for them at every opportunity is a good example of an expressive voter. Pat is typical of this type of voter. Another example would be someone who likes the Greens, knows they have very little chance of winning, but still votes Green, as a signal to politics watchers that there are voters who agree with the Greens' views. The expression of feeling for the party is more important than playing a part in choosing the MP, so the aim is to express a view regardless of its electoral impact. Selective voters are more interested in helping to choose the winner and so will concentrate their choice on those candidates who they believe are in the running. The accuracy of this informa-tion is not important, so even if someone votes for a candidate who ends up in fourth place, if the voter thought that candidate had a chance of success and was influenced by that idea, then that person is a selective voter. If Simon votes for Labour because he thinks the two most likely winners are Labour and the Conservatives, then he is being selective even if in the end Labour comes third.

Table 5.2 Perceptions of the voting decision

Primary motivation	Aim of the vote	
	Expression	Selection
Positive	supporters	choosers
Negative	negative voters	tactical voters

Tactical voters are a prime example of selective voters, as they are concerned to vote for whichever of the parties they think has the best chance of beating their disliked party. Another example of a selective voter is Rachel, who likes the Greens best, but decides to assess the environmentalist policies of the parties who came first and second in the last contest and vote accordingly. In each case the aim is to impact on the final outcome by concentrating on applying an assessment criterion just to the candidates who are thought to be frontrunners. Those voters who are most interested in influencing the result, and thus wanting to select from between possible winners, will react to ideas of a wasted vote, bandwagons or the tactical situation. They see the voting decision as a time to choose between the options provided, so the ways in which the choice is structured by the electoral and party systems will be crucial. Expressive voters are immune to such factors because they see the election as a chance to register how they feel, regardless of the competitive situation.

Combining these two variables gives a range of four distinct perceptions of the voting decision (see Tables 5.2 and 5.3). Voters with a positive motivation and desire to be expressive are the classic loyal partisans captured in the party identification model and properly described as supporters. Their strongest feeling is liking for a party, and they see the election as a time to register their allegiance to that party. Wendy strongly likes the Conservatives and so votes for them in every election to show her support. Combining a positive motivation with a tendency to be selective will also tend to lead to loyal voting if it is a major party that is supported, but may result in voting for a less preferred party if the favourite is a minor party. Such voters are interested in choosing between the candid-ates that they see as having a chance of success and they base their choice on how much they like each realistic contender. For example, Simon and Rachel have voted Liberal Democrat in the last two general elections, but do so because they prefer that party to the

Table 5.3 Examples of each decision type

Decision type	Vote in election for			Favourite party	Least favourite party	Name used in examples in text
	MP	MEP	Councillor			
Supporter (positive and expressive)	CON	CON	CON	CON	LAB	Wendy
Chooser (positive and selective)	LD	LD	LD	LD	CON	Simon
	LD	LAB	LAB	GR	CON	Rachel
Supporter (polarized and expressive)	LAB	LAB	LAB	LAB	CON	Pat
Chooser (polarized and selective)	CON	LD	LD	CON	LAB, GR	Joe
Negative voter (negative and expressive)	CON	CON	CON	CON	LAB	Leon
Tactical voter (negative and selective)	CON	LAB	LAB	GR	LD	Ali
	LD	LD	LAB	LAB, GR	CON	Colleen

Key: CON = Conservatives; GR = Green Party; LAB = Labour; LD = Liberal Democrats
Results at the previous election were: Conservative MP, LD close 2nd, Labour 3rd and Green lost deposit; LD MEP in close three-way race, with Labour just ahead of Conservatives and Greens 4th; Labour councillor with LD close 2nd, Greens 3rd and Conservatives distant 4th.

Conservatives and they see those two parties as the most likely winners in their constituency. Simon's favourite party is the Liberal Democrats, while Rachel thinks the Greens are the best party, followed by Labour and is neutral towards the Liberal Democrats. Both are choosers, because they want to help select the winner and only consider their preference ordering of the candidates they think are most likely to finish first and second. Simon votes Liberal Democrat in all three types of election because in each case he perceives them to be in the top two. However, Rachel votes Labour in the European and council elections because she prefers them to the Liberal Democrats, who are the other contender in these contests. Therefore, the voter's perception of the contest is vital to choosers, but irrelevant to supporters.

Those who are polarized in their relative party feeling behave in a similar way to the positive partisans. The relative party feeling measure may result in a balanced view, because strength of liking for one party is matched by equal strength of dislike for another. So Pat is an habitual supporter of Labour, regardless of the type of election, because her liking of that party is buttressed by dislike of the Conservatives, whom she thinks of as 'the enemy', and she sees the election as a time to express her opinion. Joe also has a balanced relative party feeling pattern, but sees the election in selective terms, so votes Conservative, because he prefers them to the Liberal Democrats and thinks these are the two likely contenders. But at another time, if he thought the two frontrunners were Liberal Democrat and Green, then he would vote for the former. Voters whose strongest feeling is against a party and who see the election as a time to express their feelings, are likely to vote for the party that they see as being most strongly opposed to their disliked party. One example of such a negative voter would be Leon, who votes Conservative because they are the most opposed to Labour, whom he strongly dislikes. He votes the same way at each election because he is interested in expressing a view, not choosing a winner.

Combining negative motivation with a desire to select, as described above, gives a classic tactical voter. Ali is most interested in stopping the election of the Liberal Democrats and so looks for the candidate most likely to beat them in each contest. For the general election, the Conservative seems the best option, but in the other contests he thinks Labour has a better chance of beating the Liberal Democrat candidate. Colleen, another tactical voter, wants to do everything she can to prevent Conservative candidates winning, so she votes Liberal Democrat in the general and European elections, but Labour for the council. In each case, among parties other than the one that is disliked, the perceived chances of success are more important than preference ordering. So Colleen in the European elections votes Liberal Democrat, which is her third-placed party, rather than her favourite, Labour, because she thinks the Liberal Democrat candidate has a better chance than the Labour candidate of beating the Conservative candidate.

Thus using these two variables to classify voters in terms of how they perceive the voting decision will result in categories such as 'supporter', 'chooser', 'tactical voter' and 'negative voter'. Those within each category can then be studied to find common traits that help to explain their perception of the voting decision. In other words, the assumption is that a Conservative 'supporter' may have as much, if not more, in common with a Labour 'supporter' as with a tactical voter who opted for the Conservatives at that election. Pat and Wendy, the supporters in Table 5.3, both vote for a party they strongly like in the belief that they should be standing up to be counted as followers of that party (Labour and Conservative respectively). Comparing Wendy to other Conservative voters in the examples (see Table 5.3), there is less motivational similarity. Leon also votes consistently for the Conservatives, but his main motivation is a strong dislike of Labour compared to Wendy's strong like of the Conservatives. Ali has also voted Conservative, but as a tactical move to try and prevent a Liberal Democrat victory. So the three Conservative voters in the examples cast that vote for very different reasons, only one based on attraction to the party. The three voters labelled as choosers (Simon, Rachel and Joe) between them voted Conservative, Labour and Liberal Democrat, but share a desire to make a choice based on their preference ordering of the two frontrunners. Rachel's vote for Labour in these circumstances shares more motivational aspects with Simon's vote for the Liberal Democrats than with Pat's supportive or Ali's tactical vote for Labour.

An election presents the voter with a range of candidates, most standing for a political party, and voters are expected to indicate a preference for one of those candidates. The orthodox literature assumes that it is the party label that is important and that voters are choosing the party they like best. As discussed earlier (see Chapter 2), there are a vast number of different decisions that the voter could be making. Each idea about what the voting decision

their preference order, and votes cast for losing candidates are reallocated to remaining candidates using the marked preferences, so there is no need to choose between an expressive and a selective vote. Under these systems there are different types of selective voting and the electoral system plays a major part in framing voter perceptions of the voting decision.

Greater study could be made of the cases in the UK where voters are faced with a variety of electoral systems. The most common example is voters living in local government areas where all three councillors are elected in the same year. In these elections voters mark a preference for three candidates on one ballot paper, rather than one preference in three separate years, as happens in other areas. Do voters behave differently given this option? Do they take advantage of the wider choice by giving one vote to a candidate from one of the smaller parties and thus mixing expressive and selective behaviour? The other example of a different electoral system is Northern Ireland, where STV (single transferable vote) is used for local government elections and to elect members of the European Parliament, but first-past-the-post is still used for electing MPs to the House of Commons. Northern Ireland is routinely excluded from studies of British voting behaviour because of the totally different party system. Nevertheless, a panel survey in Northern Ireland conducted by local academics, which looked at differing behaviour for the elections under different systems, may provide useful information for the wider study of electoral behaviour. Given the same party system but different constituencies and a different voting system, do the voters behave differently? Political divides are starkly drawn in Northern Ireland, providing a fascinating case study in reaction to the electoral context. Using these cases of voters reacting to a variety of electoral situations may help to explain the way that the system structures voters' perceptions of the voting decision.

The party system determines the options that a voter has. If there are only two parties, the opportunities for selective voting are removed and all voters are faced with the same choice however they see the voting decision. Presented with a choice between a Labour and a Conservative candidate, a voter will choose the preferred one regardless of whether that choice is based on strong liking of one candidate, strong dislike of the opponent, a desire to be counted as a supporter or a desire to stop the election of the disliked candidate. If there are more than two parties, the exact number of parties and their perceived chances of success will alter the type of choice open to selective voters. How parties are arrayed along significant political spectra, and the total number, will also affect the pattern of relative party feelings that voters hold for the range of parties. Both the electoral and party systems work on each other and, of course, affected previous election results. So the precise choice facing a voter at a given election is shaped by the electoral system, party system and behaviour of previous voters. The way in which the situation is presented, by the media and political parties, will also have an effect on voters' perceptions of the voting decision.

The ways in which the voting decision is created and framed will affect the ways in which it is seen by voters. Selective voters, in particular, are reacting to the specific situation in their constituency. The interplay between the party and electoral systems leads to different contests in different areas. Britain in the 1990s is increasingly seen as having two separate party systems, with the Conservatives being challenged by the Liberal Democrats in the south-west and Labour in the north-east. So the choice offered to anti-Conservative selective voters differs depending on which part of the country they live in. Other parties may do well among selective voters if they can illustrate a chance of success. Here, opinion polls and the idea of a bandwagon may play a crucial role in attracting more selective voters. So the way in which voters perceive the voting decision will also impact on the campaigning tactics of the parties. If a party receives a substantial proportion of its votes from negatively motivated voters, then it will need to use negative campaigns to remind voters why they hate 'the enemy', whereas a party that predominantly gains positive votes can concentrate on attracting people and reinforcing their ties to that party. Those parties that do well from selective voters need to maintain their position in the top two in each contest and ensure that voters know that they have a chance of winning the seat. Emphasis on the idea of a wasted vote and reminders of the result at the last election or recent opinion polls would be useful. When there is a large pool of expressive voters a smaller party may gain votes by winning over voters to its way of thinking, for example, the Greens in the 1989 European elections. So the actual contest in each area and the way in which that specific election is portrayed are important elements in studying voting behaviour. The political parties create the choices that voters face and react to the choices made by voters. Applying evidence about party reaction to the electoral context would add a useful layer of understanding to the study of voting behaviour.

British voters go to the polling booths more often than just for general elections and their behaviour at local, national and European elections seems to change in relation to the body being elected. Media coverage of local and European elections often suggests that voters are reacting to the national political situation and treat such contests as a large opinion poll on satisfaction with the government, rather than as a chance to influence the policies of the council or European Parliament.

There are other important ways in which behaviour at the different types of contest differs. Fewer people vote at local and European elections than at general elections, so questions relating to views on turnout could be investigated. Do supporters feel that these elections are another opportunity to show their support or do they abstain because they do not see the contest as an important test for the party? Are selective voters attracted to European contests because they care about who wins or are they put off because the identity of their MEP is not important to them?

There also seems to be evidence of distinct patterns of voting behaviour at different types of elections, and it is not uncommon for an area to have an MP from one party and local councillors or an MEP from another. It may be that voters perceive the voting decision in different ways for each type of election. For example, Hannah votes tactically for the Liberal Democrats in the general election because she cares passionately about the make-up of the national government and wants to ensure that the Conservatives do not win (see Table 5.4). But in the European election she casts an expressive vote for her favourite party, Labour, because she perceives MEPs as being powerless and so feels free to use her vote as a signal of support, even though she doubts Labour can win. At the local election she voted Green as a protest against a recent decision by the balanced Labour and Liberal Democrat council to build a swimming pool in the neighbouring village. Not only did Hannah vote for a different party at each election, but she also held a different view about the type of decision to be made, based on her perception of the situation. Her pattern of relative party feeling stayed the same, but her perception of the vote as a time to be selective or expressive changed according to how she viewed the different types of elected bodies. Again this is an example of the need to concentrate on what is being decided rather than why the voter now prefers a different party from the one preferred at the previous election.

Table 5.4 One person, three views of the decision

Decision type	Vote	Type of election
Tactical	Liberal Democrat	MP
Negative	Labour	MEP
Protest	Green	Councillor

Hannah is a negative partisan: she likes Labour, is neutral
to Greens and Liberal Democrats and strongly dislikes the
Conservatives.

Results at the previous election were: Conservative MP,
LD close 2nd, Labour 3rd and Green 4th; LD MEP in close
three-way race, with Labour just ahead of Conservatives
and Greens 4th; Labour councillor with LD close 2nd,
Greens 3rd and Conservatives distant 4th.

Comparing the voting behaviour of British voters at the three
levels of elections would show if the variations in outcome are due
to people voting differently or because of who turns out to vote
and the ways in which boundaries are drawn. If people are, in fact,
voting differently at the various types of elections, this should
provide fertile ground for investigation. Do people recognize the
distinctive jobs done by councillors, MPs and MEPs and so weigh
different factors when making each decision? Rather, it may be that
the variation is caused by the selective voters who see a different
pair of parties as the frontrunners in each contest. Or are the differences in behaviour related to the timing of each type of election
within the electoral cycle, with the government suffering from a
mid-term slump in local elections? In this case, changes are due to
shifts in voter perceptions of the parties rather than the situation.
If voters are making a distinct type of decision at each level of
election, then a study of voting patterns across the different types
of contest would help increase our understanding of how voters
perceive voting decisions.

A fourth, though less regular, type of decision faced by some
voters is that faced at by-elections. Such contests are notorious for
providing big upsets, especially in seats previously held by the
government. Christchurch, Mid-Staffordshire and Govan are recent
examples, but this is not a new phenomenon, as Orpington (1962),
Rochdale (1972) and Crosby (1981), to mention just a few, testify.
Such seats are usually regained by the defeated party at the subsequent general election. Thus by-elections are often seen as an

unreliable guide to public opinion. Nevertheless, they do present a different electoral decision in a very specific contest. Close academic study of a by-election can provide useful material on a specific contest in a finite area. Because a by-election is confined to one area, it is possible to study closely the campaign and the interplay of local and national factors. Rather than viewing such mass changes in behaviour as anomalies, it may be useful to make a deeper study of voter attitudes at by-elections compared to general elections, perhaps by using a panel survey and picking up by-election voters in the following general election. Instead of ignoring by-elections because they produce 'odd' results, it may be more profitable to use each as the chance to put a specific constituency contest under the microscope. Each individual study may provide new clues for unravelling the wider question of what voters decide.

Summary

Most of the suggested new focus relates to the way in which voters are studied, therefore the changes need to be adopted by academics. But where does this leave the student of voting behaviour? Because the study of voters is heavily dependent on survey data, the ways in which past surveys were conducted shape what we can investigate about past elections. Students cannot explore the type of questions suggested above in relation to the behaviour of voters in the past. All that can be done is to have an awareness of the orthodoxy when studying works contained within its doctrines. When reading the orthodox texts, ask the missing questions, be aware of other responses and, most importantly, look out for the unstated assumptions.

The assumption that a vote is a sign of support is fundamental to the orthodox approach, so changing the focus to look at what voters are deciding marks a total shift in emphasis. It implies moving from a study of vote choice with party as the dependent variable to an analysis of different types of decisions with type of behaviour as the dependent variable. Looking at groups of voters who behave in a particular way is central to a focus on what voters decide. Rather than dismissing the atypical as anomalies, one should see that their very atypicality within the existing models makes them interesting. For instance, habitual choosers or tactical voters clearly see the voting decision as something other than a sign of support. Accepting that voters make different types of decisions is rejecting the idea that all voting behaviour can be explained by looking at general trends

across time and place with one model. A change in focus to the
types of decisions made by voters would entail some micro-analysis.

If we want to know about the range of decisions voters see themselves making, then we have to look at individual cases first to build
up the relevant groups. Developing micro-analyses and taking a
narrower scope is relevant for a detailed study of perceptions of the
voting decision. At the same time, the election has to be put into
context. The choice presented to voters is affected by the electoral
and party systems and the events both at the last election and
in politics since then. So the choice faced by voters needs to be considered as part of an ongoing political process. Elections are seen as
vitally important in shaping government and thus an action that
takes about a minute is analysed in great detail. But the vote could
also be seen as just another decision taken by people who make
choices all of the time, and know they will have to make political
choices again in the future. A concentration on the decision
making rather than the political aspects of an election recognizes
this perspective.

Bibliography

Abramson, P. R., Aldrich, J. H., Paolino, P. and Rhode, D. W. (1992) 'Sophisticated' voting in the 1988 Presidential primaries. *American Political Science Review*, **89**: 55–69.

Aimer, P. (1989) Travelling together: party identification and voting in the New Zealand general election of 1987. *Electoral Studies*, **8**: 131–42.

Baron, R. A. and Byrne, D. (1984) *Social Psychology: Understanding Human Interaction*, 4th edn. Boston: Allyn and Bacon.

Baxter, R. D. (1866) *The Re-distribution of Seats and the Counties*. London: Edward Stamford.

Bean, C., McAllister, I. and Warhurst, J. (1990) *The Greening of Australian Politics: The 1990 Federal Election*. Melbourne: Longman-Cheshire.

Beck, P. A., Baum, L., Clausen, A. R. and Smith, C. E., Jr. (1992) Patterns and sources of ticket splitting in subpresidential voting. *American Political Science Review*, **86**: 916–28.

Benney, M., Gray, A. P. and Pear, R. H. (1956) *How People Vote*. London: Routledge.

Berelson, B. R., Lazarsfeld, P. F. and McPhee, W. N. (1954) *Voting: A Study of Opinion Formation in a Presidential Campaign*. Chicago: University of Chicago Press.

Berrington, H. B. (1965) The general election of 1964. *Journal of the Royal Statistical Society*, **128**: 17–51.

Bishop, G. F., Tuchfarber, A. J. and Oldendick, R. W. (1986) Opinions on fictitious issues: the pressure to answer survey questions. *Public Opinion Quarterly*, **50**: 240–50.

Blake, D. (1982) The consistency of 'inconsistency': party identification in Canada. *Canadian Journal of Political Science*, **15**: 691–710.

Bodman, A. R. (1983) The neighbourhood effect: a test of the Butler–Stokes model. *British Journal of Political Science*, **13**: 243–9.

Bowler, S. (1990a) Consistency and inconsistency in Canadian party identifications: towards an institutional approach. *Electoral Studies*, **9**: 133–45.

Bowler, S. (1990b) Voter perceptions and party strategies. *Comparative Politics*, **22**: 61–83.

Bowler, S. and Denemark, D. (1993) Split ticket voting in Australia:

deraignment and inconsistent votes reconsidered. *Australian Journal of Political Science*, **28**: 19–37.

Bowler, S. and Farrell, D. M. (1991) Party loyalties in complex settings: STV and party identification. *Political Studies*, **39**: 350–62.

Bowler, S. and Lanoue, D. J. (1992) Strategic and protest voting for third parties: the case of the Canadian NDP. *Western Political Quarterly*, **45**: 485–99.

Butler, D. (1951) *The British General Election of 1951*. London: Macmillan.

Butler, D. (1955) *The British General Election of 1955*. London: Macmillan.

Butler, D. (1965) Discussion of Berrington on the general election of 1964. *The Journal of the Royal Statistical Society*, **128**: 51–2.

Butler, D. and Kavanagh, D. (1979) *The British General Election of 1979*. London: Macmillan.

Butler, D. and Kavanagh, D. (1988) *The British General Election of 1987*. London: Macmillan.

Butler, D. and Kavanagh, D. (1992) *The British General Election of 1992*. London: Macmillan.

Butler, D. and King, A. (1966) *The British General Election of 1966*. London: Macmillan.

Butler, D. and Stokes, D. (1969) *Political Change in Britain*. London: Macmillan.

Butler, D. and Stokes, D. (1974) *Political Change in Britain*, 2nd edn. London: Macmillan.

Campbell, A., Converse, P. E., Miller, W. E. and Stokes, D. E. (1960) *The American Voter*. New York: Wiley.

Campbell, A., Converse, P. E., Miller, W. E. and Stokes, D. E. (1964) *The American Voter: An Abridgment*. New York: John Wiley & Sons.

Catt, H. (1989) Tactical voting in Britain. *Parliamentary Affairs*, **42**: 548–59.

Catt, H. (1990) Individual behaviour versus collective outcomes: the case of tactical voting. *Politics*, **10**: 17–24.

Chambers Twentieth Century Dictionary (1977) London: Chambers.

Converse, P. (1976) *The Dynamics of Party Support: Cohort Analyzing Party Identification*. Newbury Park, CA: Sage.

Cornford, J. R., Dobling, D. F. L. and Tether, B. S. (1995) Historical precedent and British electoral prospects. *Electoral Studies*, **14**: 123–42.

Cox, G. W. (1986) The development of a party-oriented electorate in England, 1832–1918. *British Journal of Political Science*, **16**: 187–216.

Crewe, I., Fox, T. and Alt, J. (1977) Non-voting in British general elections 1966–October 1974. *British Political Sociology Yearbook*, **3**: 38–109.

Crewe, I. and Norris, P. (1992) In defence of British electoral studies. In Crewe, I. *et al.* (eds), *British Elections and Parties Yearbook 1991*. London: Harvester Wheatsheaf.

Curtice, J. and Steed, M. (1982) Electoral choice and the production of government. *British Journal of Political Science*, **12**: 249–99.

Curtice, J. and Steed, M. (1988) Analysis. In Butler, D. and Kavanagh, D., *The British General Election of 1987*. London: Macmillan, pp. 316–62.

Denver, D. (1989) *Elections and Voting Behaviour in Britain*. London: Philip Allan.

Denver, D. and Hands, G. (1985) Marginality and turnout in general elections in the 1970s. *British Journal of Political Science*, **15**: 381–8.

Denver, D. and Hands, G. (1992) *Issues and Controversies in British Electoral Behaviour*. London: Harvester Wheatsheaf.

Downs, A. (1957) *An Economic Theory of Democracy*. New York: Harper.

Drake, M. (1971) The mid-Victorian voter. *Journal of Interdisciplinary History*, **1**: 473–90.

Dunleavy, P. (1979) The urban basis of political alignment: social class, domestic property ownership and state intervention in consumption processes. *British Journal of Political Science*, **9**: 409–43.

Dunleavy, P. (1987) Class dealignment in Britain revisited. *West European Politics*, **10**: 400–20.

Dunleavy, P. (1990) Mass political behaviour: is there more to learn? *Political Studies*, **38**: 453–69.

Dunleavy, P. and Husbands, C. T. (1985) *British Democracy at the Crossroads*. London: George Allen and Unwin.

Dunleavy, P., Gamble, A. and Peele, G. (1990) *Developments in British Politics 3*. London: Macmillan.

Duverger, M. (1986) Duverger's law forty years later. In Grofman, B. and Lijphart, A. (eds), *Electoral Laws and their Political Consequences*. New York: Agathon Press.

Eagles, E. (1992) Sources of variation in working class formation: ecological, sectoral and socialization influences. *European Journal of Political Research*, **21**: 225–43.

Eagles, M. and Erfle, J. (1989) Community cohesion and voter turnout in English parliamentary constituencies. *British Journal of Political Science*, **19**: 115–25.

Fiorina, M. P. (1981) *Retrospective Voting in American National Elections*. London: Yale University Press.

Fiske, S. T. (1980) Attention and weight in person perception: the impact of negative and extreme behaviour. *Journal of Personality and Social Psychology*, **38**: 889–906.

Fitton, M. (1973) Neighbourhood and voting: a sociometric examination. *British Journal of Political Science*, **3**: 445–72.

Franklin, M. N. (1985) *The Decline of Class Voting in Britain: Changes in the Basis of Electoral Choice, 1964–1983*. Oxford: Clarendon Press.

Galbraith, J. W. and Rae, N. C. (1989) A test of the importance of tactical voting: Great Britain, 1987. *British Journal of Political Science*, **19**: 126–38.

Gidengil, E. (1992) Canada votes: a quarter century of Canadian national election surveys. *Canadian Journal of Political Science*, **25**: 217–48.

Granberg, D. and Holmberg, S. (1991) Election campaign volatility in Sweden and the United States. *Electoral Studies*, **10**: 208–30.

Grunberg, G. (1988) Recent developments in French electoral sociology. *Electoral Studies*, **7**: 3–14.

Harrop, M. and Miller, W. L. (1987) *Elections and Voters: A Comparative Introduction*. London: Macmillan.

Heath, A. and Pierce, R. (1992) It was party identification all along: question order effects of reports of party identification in Britain. *Electoral Studies*, **11**: 93–105.

Heath, A., Jowell, R. and Curtice, J. (1985) *How Britain Votes*. Oxford: Pergamon Press.

Heath, A., Jowell, R., Curtice, J., Evans, G., Field, J. and Witherspoon, S. (1991) *Understanding Political Change*. Oxford: Pergamon Press.

Himmelweit, H. T., Humphreys, P. and Jaeger, M. (1985) *How Voters Decide*. Milton Keynes: Open University Press.

Hippler, H. J. and Schwarz, N. (1986) Not forbidding isn't allowing: the cognitive basis of the forbid–allow asymmetry. *Public Opinion Quarterly*, **50**: 89–96.

Huckfeldt, R. and Sprague, J. (1991) Discussant effects on vote choice. *Journal of Politics*, **53**: 122–58.

Jackson, F. J., Jr. (1992) How uncertain terms affect survey data. *Public Opinion Quarterly*, **56**: 218–31.

Jesse, E. (1988) Split-voting in the Federal Republic of Germany: an analysis of the Federal elections from 1953 to 1987. *Electoral Studies*, **7**: 109–24.

Jesse, E. (1990) *Elections: the Federal Republic of Germany in Comparison*. Oxford: Berg.

Johnston, R. (1992) Party identification measures in the Anglo-American democracies: a national survey experiment. *American Journal of Political Science*, **36**: 542–59.

Johnston, R. J. and Pattie, C. J. (1991) Tactical voting in Great Britain in 1983 and 1987: an alternative approach. *British Journal of Political Science*, **21**: 95–109.

Johnston, R., Blais, A., Brady, H. E. and Crete, J. (1992) *Letting the People Decide: Dynamics of a Canadian Election*. Stanford: Stanford University Press.

Johnston, R. J., Pattie, C. J. and Allsopp, J. G. (1988) *A Nation Dividing?* London: Longman.

Kinder, D. R. and Kiewiet, R. (1981) Sociotropic politics: the American case. *British Journal of Political Science*, **11**: 129–61.

Lazarsfeld, P. F., Berelson, B. and Gaudet, H. (1948) *The People's Choice: How the Voter Makes up his Mind in a Presidential Campaign*, 2nd edn. New York: Columbia University Press.

Linton, M. (ed.) (1992) *The Guide to the House of Commons*. London: Fourth Estate.

Listhaug, O. (1989) *Citizens, Parties and Norwegian Electoral Politics 1957–1985: An Empirical Study*. Trondheim: Tapir.

Lutz, J. M. (1981) The spread of the Plaid Cymru: the spatial impress. *Western Political Quarterly*, **34:** 310–28.

Lutz, J. M. (1986) Community context in the spread of voter support for the Scottish Nationalist Party. *Western Political Quarterly*, **39:** 455–63.

MacKuen, M. and Brown, C. (1987) Political context and attitude change. *American Political Science Review*, **81:** 471–90.

Marcus, G. E. and MacKuen, M. B. (1993) Anxiety, enthusiasm and the vote. *American Political Science Review*, **87:** 672–85.

Martin, J. B. (1874) The elections of 1868 and 1874. *Statistical Society Journal*, **67:** 193–225.

McAllister, I. and Darcy, R. (1992) Sources of split-ticket voting in the 1988 American elections. *Political Studies*, **40:** 695–712.

McAllister, I. and Studlar, D. T. (1992) Region and voting in Britain 1979–87: territorial polarization or artifact? *American Journal of Political Science*, **36:** 168–99.

McAllister, I. and Wattenberg, M. (1995) Measuring levels of party identification. *Public Opinion Quarterly*, **59:** 259–68.

McIlroy, J. (1989) Trade unions and the law. In Jones, B. (ed.), *Political Issues in Britain Today*. Manchester: Manchester University Press.

McKenzie, P. T. and Silver, A. (1968) *Angels in Marble: Working Class Conservatives in Urban England*. London: Heinmann Educational.

McLean, I. (1980) *Elections*, 2nd edn. London: Longman.

Middendorp, C. P. and Tanke, P. R. K. (1990) Economic voting in the Netherlands. *European Journal of Political Research*, **18:** 535–55.

Miller, A. H. and Wlezien, C. (1993) The social group dynamics of partisan evaluations. *Electoral Studies*, **12:** 5–22.

Miller, A. H., Wlezien, C. and Hildreth, A. (1991) A reference group theory of partisan coalitions. *Journal of Politics*, **91:** 1134–49.

Miller, W. L. (1977) *Electoral Dynamics in Britain Since 1918*. London: Macmillan.

Miller, W. L. (1978) Social class and party choice in England: a new analysis. *British Journal of Political Science*, **8:** 257–84.

Miller, W. L., Clarke, H. D., Harrop, M., Leduc, L. and Whiteley, P. F. (1990) *How Voters Change: The 1987 British Election Campaign in Perspective*. Oxford: Clarendon Press.

Milne, R. S. and MacKenzie, H. C. (1958) *Marginal Seat*. London: Hansard Society.

Newmarch, W. (1857) On the electoral statistics of the counties and boroughs in England and Wales during 25 years from the Reform Act of 1832 to the present day. *Statistical Society Journal*, **20:** 169–234.

Niemi, R. G., Whitten, G. and Franklin, M. N. (1992) Constituency characteristics, individual characteristics and tactical voting in the 1987 British general election. *British Journal of Political Science*, **22:** 229–54.

Nordlinger, E. A. (1967) *The Working Class Tories: Authority, Deference and Stable Democracy*. London: MacGibbon and Kee.

Owens, J. R. and Wade, L. L. (1988) Economic conditions and constituency voting in Great Britain. *Political Studies*, **36**: 30–51.

Oxford English Dictionary (1993) Oxford: Clarendon Press.

Parkin, F. (1968) *Middle Class Radicalism: The Social Bases of the British Campaign for Nuclear Disarmament*. Manchester: Manchester University Press.

Pomper, G. M. (1988) *Voters, Elections and Parties*. Oxford: Transaction Books.

Powell, G. B., Jr. and Whitten, G. D. (1993) A cross-national analysis of economic voting. *American Journal of Political Science*, **37**: 391–414.

Presser, S. and Traugott, M. (1992) Little white lies and social science models. *Public Opinion Quarterly*, **56**: 77–86.

Putnam, R. D. (1966) Political attitudes and the local community. *American Political Science Review*, **60**: 640–54.

Rahn, W. M. (1993) The role of partisan stereotypes in information processing about political candidates. *American Journal of Political Science*, **37**: 479–96.

Rasmussen, J. (1965) The disutility of the swing concept in British psephology. *Parliamentary Affairs*, **18**: 442–54.

Rasmussen, J. (1973) The impact of constituency structural characteristics upon political preferences in Britain. *Comparative Politics*, **6**: 123–46.

Rawlings, H. F. (1988) *Law and the Electoral Process*. London: Sweet & Maxwell.

Rose, R. and McAllister, I. (1986) *Voters Begin to Choose*. London: Sage Publications.

Sanchez, M. E. (1992) Effects of questionnaire design on the quality of survey data. *Public Opinion Quarterly*, **56**: 206–17.

Sarlvik, B. and Crewe, I. (1983) *Decade of Dealignment*. London: Cambridge University Press.

Scarbrough, E. (1984) *Political Ideology and Voting: An Exploratory Study*. Oxford: Clarendon Press.

Scarbrough, E. (1987) The British electorate twenty years on: electoral change and the election surveys. *British Journal of Political Science*. **17**: 219–46.

Schreiber, E. M. (1975) Dirty data in Britain and the USA: the reliability of 'invariant' characteristics reported in surveys. *Public Opinion Quarterly*, **39**: 493–506.

Schuman, H. (1986) Ordinary questions, survey questions and policy questions. *Public Opinion Quarterly*, **50**: 432–42.

Schuman, H. and Presser, S. (1981) *Questions and Answers in Attitude Surveys: Experiments on Question Form, Wording and Context*. New York: Academic Press.

Schwarz, N., Knauper, B., Hippler, H. J., Noelle-Neuman, E. and Clark, L. (1991) Rating scales: numeric values may change the meaning of scale labels. *Public Opinion Quarterly*, **55**: 570–82.

Singer, E. (1988) Pushing back the limits to surveys. *Public Opinion Quarterly*, **52:** 416–26.

Smith, T. W. (1987) That which we call welfare by any other name would smell sweeter: an analysis of the impact of question wording on response patterns. *Public Opinion Quarterly*, **51:** 75–83.

Swaddle, K. and Heath, A. (1989) Official and reported turnout in the British general election of 1987. *British Journal of Political Science*, **19:** 537–50.

Tourangeau, R., Rasinski, K. A., Bradburn, N. and D'Andrade, R. (1989) Carryover effects in attitude surveys. *Public Opinion Quarterly*, **53:** 495–524.

Wilcox, C., Sigelman, L. and Cook, E. (1989) Some like it hot: individual differences in responses to group feeling thermometers. *Public Opinion Quarterly*, **53:** 246–57.

Zaller, J. and Feldman, S. (1992) A simple theory of the survey response. *American Journal of Political Science*, **36:** 579–616.

Name Index

Subject Index